PRAISE FOR *LOVE ME TO LIFE*

In reviewing this manuscript, I was impressed by the passion and experience of this author. Her interviewing of various ministry leaders, counselors and others was excellent. Her process itself opens conversations that many would prefer to avoid, both within the church and without. To take that process to stakeholders was very creative and important. By seeking both survivors of suicide attempts and family members and others close to the individual, she brings a perspective that is important to first responders, chaplains, counselors and ministry leaders. I was particularly impressed by her advocacy for training of congregation members to serve as back-up support. ...

This work should be used by Chaplains and other ministers who wish to equip believers in Crisis Ministry. It will also be valuable reading for those who have either survived suicide attempt or been close to survivors. They will gain great insights into the thoughts and concerns of people affected by these crises, especially as they read of Veronica's personal experiences.

Greg Linnebach, DMin
Primus University of Theology International
Phoenix, AZ

This book has been very convicting!

Veronica has done an amazing job presenting the case for an area she is gifted in and passionate about improving. The research contained here shows compelling evidence of needed resources and help from the local church that is lacking. I know we can do more! Much more needs to be done to help in the areas of suicide and other traumatic events that are so devastating to family and friends.

I have recently survived two tragic family deaths within a single year's time. One an accident, and the other a suicide that caught us completely off guard. The pain is real, and good resources and available help are way too scarce.

Billy Beacham

Teaching pastor at First Baptist Church, Burleson, Texas
President of Student Discipleship Ministries, which provides
spiritual growth resources for all ages and houses the offices for
See You at the Pole, the largest global student prayer movement in
history.

Love Me to Life

Suicide Recovery at Church

Veronica Sites

Energion Publications
Gonzalez, Florida
2020

Unless otherwise noted, Scripture taken from the NEW AMERI-
CAN STANDARD BIBLE(R), Copyright (C) 1960,1962,1963,
1968,1971,1972,1973,1975,1977,1995 by The Lockman Foundation. Used by permission.

Cover Design: Christine Dupre, www.Vidagraphicdesign.com

ISBN: 978-1-63199-736-5
eISBN: 978-1-63199-737-2

Library of Congress Control Number: 2020951064

Energion Publications
P. O. Box 841
Gonzalez, FL 32560

energion.com
pubs@energion.com

TABLE OF CONTENTS

Introduction.. 1
    Laying Foundations to Improve Ministry
    to Persons Impacted by Suicide 3
    Questioning Ministry 7
    Divine Diversity.. 27
    Stewardship Of Wellness 43
    Mystery Of The Unknown 61
    Hindsight Help 79

Part One: Identifying Trends 89
    Introduction to Part One 91
    Responses.. 99

Part Two: Scripture and Suicide 117
    Biblical Guidance.. 119
    Addressing Suicide 131
    Practicalities 135

Part Three: Triumph Over Tragedy
    — A Personal Testimony 143
    Crisis Response Process 145
    Personal Testimony — My Crisis.............................. 157
    Post-Trauma Growth 187

Appendix I 199
Appendix II... 207
Appendix III.. 209
Appendix IV.. 213

Bibliography.. 219
Scripture Index... 231

INTRODUCTION

Laying Foundations To Improve Ministry to Persons Impacted by Suicide

When it comes to crisis, there is a gap between ministry education and life's real-time demands. This gap results in on-the-job training, which can leave both the one ministering and the one being ministered to feeling inadequate, discouraged, and defeated. Too often, unless a need necessitates consideration and demands attention, answers to questions asked remain unanswered or avoided until tensions or a crisis pass. Many leaders are aware of a specific proverbial "elephant in the foyer" that exists in churches of all sizes, but do not know what to do about it. Some ask: How do we, as leaders, better pastor the people without compromise to good standing and reputation? How can we increase the kingdom more practically, working through awkward, stigmatized, or taboo situations?

It is time to speak up and storm the gates of hell with straightforward truths and considerations as to how leaders can increase the effectiveness of the kingdom's impact through the church. For far too long, lies have been believed. Fear hinders ministry to wounded souls, who end up leaving the church disillusioned, doubtful, and feeling forsaken.

How much, if any, seminary training is actually delivered concerning how to prepare for crisis and then minister to people when crisis occurs? We ignore this question, assuming that preparedness is already taking place. History shows that it is not. Church leaders are held to a high standard. Knowing this, ministers, be they clergy or laity, are often erroneously assumed to be skilled beyond their actual capabilities. Yet, from years of field experience as a chaplain within first responder culture, a deep conviction has compelled me to write this book. Well aware of a deficiency in such preparation, and the increasing demand in need to help people in crisis, this publication presents well-researched awareness, relevant solutions, and a call to action.

The ministry of presence, while very comforting, carries with it a need for what all leaders must get better at: self-care. The aftermath of any level of crisis leaves residual and sometimes health-compromising impact in those providing ministry. Church members must be discipled in how to tend sheep holistically so that the whole becomes stronger.

The Stewardship of Wellness is a concept introduced and confronted here because even in Bible colleges, there is little preparation for the inevitable death notification that admittedly some pray will not come to pass in the career of one's ministry. Still, unless the student thinks to ask a mentor beforehand, the need to know many "how to's" will only become evident at the hour needed, and then it is baptism by fire. Ministry leadership must be proactive.

In many cases, emergency preparedness within churches is reactionary. Prior to COVID-19, security had become increasingly heightened in effort to mitigate mass shooting incidents. The need for this action was recognized by vigilant church leaders and members. Equally as important, we must evaluate the value of a ministry of presence and the support that is needed after a wide range of crises and disasters that occur. Leaders may hope and believe they will be raptured before the tribulation; however, that hope must come with preparation. This book provides answers as to what can be done to equip the church to be a more effective and present help when the distressed seek support. It *will* happen. So how can the church do better in, during, and following a crisis?

We must call the proverbial elephant lurking among every congregation what it is. The "elephant" in congregational foyers is the subject of suicide. It can no longer remain a known presence and avoided. Too many in the community and surrounding believers worldwide are devastated by suicide and need vital ministry. A form of recovery ministry biblically founded, peer-supported, and no longer skirted around or passed off to others without ministry involvement is crucial. It is time to start the conversation with tough questions and discussions about what to do to minister more effectively in the wake of today's crisis. The church has biblical answers that must be explored by leading and discernment from the Holy Spirit. It is no secret among ministry leaders that there is a tremendous need to know how to minister to hushed and anguished souls in need of brotherly love. The stigma and shame associated with the suicide crisis no longer have a place among the body of Christ. May the betterment of ministry be the result of what the Holy Spirit does as you press on to the end.

QUESTIONING MINISTRY

For this very reason, make every effort to add to your faith goodness; and to goodness, knowledge; ⁶ and to knowledge, self-control; and to self-control, perseverance; and to perseverance, godliness; ⁷ and to godliness, mutual affection; and to mutual affection, love. ⁸ For if you possess these qualities in increasing measure, they will keep you from being ineffective and unproductive in your knowledge of our Lord Jesus Christ. ⁹ But whoever does not have them is nearsighted and blind, forgetting that they have been cleansed from their past sins.

— 2 Peter 1:5-9

G ood leaders use the art of asking great thought-provoking questions[1] to incite human response. Brought into the church, implementing a "questioning ministry" will ignite within an individual a desire that prompts a search for answers. There is no better example of one who led with questions than Jesus during His earthly ministry. Let it be clear that by using the term "questioning ministry," I do not mean critical interrogation; rather, it is the art of asking questions that stir curiosity. What a marvelous strategy! It moves the soul and naturally launches the human spirit on a quest for answers. It is the essence of the Lord's command to ask, seek, and knock, which Scripture tells us to ask and knock so that doors may be opened. A questioning ministry sets revelation

---

1   (et. al Maxwell) "The following is true only when you are willing to ask the question. 'The ability to ask the right question is more than half of the battle of finding the answer.' The basic principle is that a profound question leads to a profound answer." The failure to look within will result in doing without what is meant to help us grow.

into motion; the opportunity for doors to open, so we learn great and marvelous things we do not, at the moment of inquiry, know.[2] This is an essential part of a believer's life, since growth and maturity are intended to be continual. Therefore, it behooves leaders to consider their attitudes and mindset concerning crisis ministry in general and more specifically the suicide crisis. After all, Christ's mission of redemption was in fact conflict resolution to humanity's greatest crisis: sin. Indeed, in this world, we face many troubles, but we have the promise and proof that Christ has overcome, and so shall we. Throughout the gospels, there are no less than three hundred thirty-nine questions[3] that model excellent leadership. Knowing His creation best, Christ appealed to our human nature, which has an innate need that begs for answers. A seeker will search to reconcile a question, motivated by a hunger to learn what it does not know, nor may have even considered, had the question not been asked in the first place.

Think of a time you wished a particular situation had been addressed in preparation for ministry. It is a vulnerable and intimidating moment of reality when everything learned in Bible college or at seminary falls short, and the person in need stands before you, awaiting direction. Ignorance, on such occasions, is not bliss. Ignorance does, however, fuel God-chasing moments in urgent prayer. In hot pursuit of help, truth, and practical application of brotherly love, a motivated minister launches his prayers heavenward in an earnest inquiry for guidance. "Holy Spirit, help!" The entire Trinity

---

2   Jeremiah 33:3 *"Call to me and I will answer you and tell you great and unsearchable things you do not know."*

3   Matthew has one hundred nine questions, Mark includes sixty-eight, Luke one hundred seven, (107), and John has fifty-five (55). Let it not be missed the life altering question asked of Paul by the risen and ascended Christ in Acts 9:4. "Who are you, Lord?" is an exemplary inquiry from Saul, who at the time was an influential leader, yet not having experienced conversion in that moment. Saul's response demonstrates the principle of ask and seek. Christ's response exemplifies the truth of revelation through inquiry. "I am Jesus... (Acts 9:5). (et.al Tiede)

is summoned to render aid and impart wisdom to help someone who cries out in hope or desperation.

In overwhelming and life-altering moments, a congregant often turns to pastoral care in hopes of obtaining wisdom and direction to stabilize the crisis. How does a pastor lead through a crisis? Whether it is a global pandemic or an individual catastrophic life event, crisis ministry is in pressing need of evaluation. COVID-19 has impacted every institution that exists. The result spiritually seems to be that the church remains active and serves others all over the world as it should always be. Still, in light of this current disaster and historical data on disaster,[4] phases of disaster must include recovery. What do emergency preparedness, knowledge of the phases of disaster, and Scripture's teaching on end times have to do with the lessons we could learn from this most recent pandemic?

---

4   "Symptoms of distress were found not only in people in the regions closest to the attack sites, but also in those located far from the attack sites, which indicates that there was no relevant proximity effect for PTSD. Accordingly, data from US residents who were indirectly exposed to the attacks showed a similar prevalence of PTSD as those who were directly exposed. Therefore, the 9/11 terror attacks could have had a profound impact on mental health worldwide." (et. al Mendenwald)

"Suicide rates may be affected by world news. Our objective was to investigate the possible impact of the terrorist attacks of September 11, 2001, on suicidal behavior in the Netherlands. There was evidence of an increase in rates of suicide and deliberate self-harm in the weeks immediately following the attacks" (et. al Lange)

Such combined historical findings point to reasonable risk factors exist and recorded as linked to the trauma of terrorism. The common denominator to an unfolding pandemic is the traumatic impact of mortality rates. Stressors resulting from mortality surrounding the Covid pandemic are complicated grief for the survivors unable to be with loved one in final hours. Add to that demographic the professional community of responders taxed by the moral challenges and injuries resulting from shortage of equipment among prioritizing care when so many flooded the healthcare system. The risk, threat, and toll on overall mental health begs the question - what long term possibilities might it behoove leaders to prepare for concerning hope and help already is needed and yet to be sought where crisis ministry is concerned?

We must consider and ask some tough "how" questions? How might the cumulative toll of a pandemic's extended period of stressors due to fluidity and unpredictable outlook impact the risk of lives lost for lack of support incrementally as the situation unfolds? What do personal crises and historical insight into the residual impact of traumatic incidents indicate we would be wise to consider planning for future ministry? How is this relevant concerning suicide prevention? The forthcoming content represents a broad spectrum of perspectives from those with lived experience, evidence-based research, and, most important, Scripture. Be advised that the content unapologetically prompts discussions to incite leaders and survivors' actions to be more proactive and collaboratively involved in suicide prevention. The church and her people must be ready to pierce the darkness with hope and help. The challenge is set.

READY OR NOT

The significant questions we must resolve for such a time as this are:

Is leadership ready for what is yet to be?

How can we, as a body of believers, be better prepared biblically and practically from lessons we have learned with the certainty of the Second Coming of Christ?

Will the church become bolder to face existing giants like suicide and the stigma that surrounds the moral injury of suicide?

We must. The facts show that this stigma surrounding suicide hinders ministry to those impacted by such devastation. Are we ready to face it? The challenge is to *be* the church we are called to be. People do not arrive at a point of ending their lives on a whim. While desperation and other factors may contribute to the act, the church would do well to take responsibility for prevention. The stigma surrounding suicide is problematic, and a giant which the church needs to face at a spiritual level. It can no longer remain an elephant in the room. Believers must abide in the certainty that the return of Christ is imminent, and in the meantime, we are his witnesses for better or for worse. Semantically, throughout this recent pandemic in which we have had to stay at home, the message that we are "living in uncertain times" has fed and increased stressors otherwise unseen. The world's experience and struggle with social distancing is counterculture to our innate humanness. We can anticipate residual impacts from this pandemic and have already experienced what is seen in other natural disasters: disgruntled victims and desperate, malcontented behavior.[5]

Consider Scripture's historical, prophetic fulfilments that led to the building of the church. In light of this, what can we anticipate needs for leading concerning eschatology? If we focus our attention on the church's role in fulfilling the great commission, we must ask: How are we doing in discipleship? With the ongoing effect of sin—the first global crisis—it may be surprising to learn some things about disasters and the predictable phasic progression involved. There are similarities that, as leaders, should drive us to be motivated to consider how we equip the saints practically for

---

5   (et al. Pulido) https://doi.org/10.1007/s10615-012-0384-3 As we near twenty years since the terrorist attacks of Sep- tember 11, 2001, much has come to light documenting evidence that direct exposure is not the only contributing factor producing victims of traumatic stress. Victimization has a "ripple effect," spreading out to all those with whom they have intimate contact (Remer and Ferguson 1995). The impact of exposure to others' pain and indirect exposures to the specific traumatic occurrence. It could be "via close contact with the survivor, retraumatization of individuals that may experience similar symptoms as a survivor of the direct and current situation. "This process has been called Secondary Traumatic Stress (STS) or Compassion Fatigue (et al. Figley)." It seems quite possible that the extended period of impact and ongoing losses whereby loved one's may not have sufficient end of life closer due to social distancing and death's occurring during the pandemic and the sudden loss of deaths by suicides may have the similarity of complex grief that must be considered as the church resumes gathering as a congregation. Much has transpired in people as time has passed and some will return with wounds that may not have had the opportunity to address or fresh although much time and transition has occurred for others. The effects of trauma have a way of sticking.

the present and future. Are we equipping one another with what is needed to persevere?

When it comes to Military Defense, the Department of Homeland Security, even at the local level, emergency management starts with preparedness. Their efforts do not end until recovery is complete. Christ will return, marking our completion and role in a collaborative mission. However, have we given consideration to what "making ready" looks like for that event beyond evangelism? The command to make disciples includes teaching *all* that Jesus commanded. We are the Lord's army. We are messengers with security who have been given orders to make disciples that are to be ready in season and out of season and for any eventuality. How are we doing?

DISASTERS AND DIVINITY

There are some parallels in the phase progressions of a hurricane that can help illustrate how we respond to a crisis. We will place in juxtaposition how ministry can strategically equip and disciple in the *Stewardship of Wellness* and *Stewardship of Mind* as both pertain to endurance and perseverance. We have the promise of perseverance of the saint. With that promise, we also need to know how to counter, endure, and overcome the enemy's attack on sound minds during trying times.

PREDICTABLE PHASES OF DISASTER

In a disaster like a hurricane, the range of impact on people rises from social and community wellbeing, individual psychological wellbeing, and public confidence. A threat to a community occurs first, followed by a warning. Psychological wellbeing remains relatively steady until the time of the event, or when a storm makes landfall. From the point of critical impact onward, psychological wellbeing takes a hit and may slump, but quickly rises as a heroic phase of response provides much needed support from responders and volunteers providing hope and help. The response climbs to a pinnacle, the honeymoon phase which brings with it elevated public confidence. The confidence feeds on itself, resulting in mass response and the presence of support from neighbors, volunteers, and vocational professionals. The hope and help coming from many sources elevates mental wellbeing through the efforts of those involved in search and rescue and recovery.

HONEYMOON

During the honeymoon phase, which is short-lived, there starts a gradual decline of wellbeing, as residents of the community feel the impact personally and realize the loss of property or life. Hope wanes when hope is deferred for assistance, rebuilding, or having the ability to find a different "normal," and this brings disillusionment. When recovery and reconstruction do begin, the plummet to social and community wellbeing will reverse. Although pending anniversaries of a disaster[6] can again cause a decline in wellbeing, a gradual climb will occur when individuals and communities settle into a different normal.

---

6   "As the anniversary of a disaster or traumatic event approaches, many survivors report a return of restlessness and fear. The anniversary reaction can involve several days or even weeks of anxiety, anger, nightmares, flashbacks, depression, or fear. On a more positive note, the anniversary of a disaster or traumatic event also can provide an opportunity for emotional healing. Not all survivors experience an anniversary reaction. However, those who do may be troubled because they did not expect and do not understand their reaction. For these individuals, knowing what to expect in advance may be helpful." (et al. American et al. 2002, OMH 2020)

As suggested, this is where ministry collaboration has the opportunity to improve. Be it a loss of life, homestead, or sense of security, life threats affect people mentally, emotionally, psychologically, spiritually, and behaviorally. Ministry is essential.

Disillusionment

How quickly or slowly it takes for reconstruction efforts to establish a stable environment impacts one's overall wellbeing. When there has been disillusionment on account of expectations surrounding reconstruction, it can take weeks, months, and even years to make progress. A predominant factor keeping one from moving from disillusionment into recovery has to do with the amount of collateral damage. The psychological impact of moving ahead from survival, to stability, to success of living beyond the event and into the significance and meaning adopted concerning the event happens over time. Sometimes the psychological impact goes uncorrelated to an event that threatened life and one's sense of security. Trauma stress is more common and less dealt with as mitigative to one's overall wellbeing. It should be handled in a manner that is not only practical, but bears a biblical model. It is from this ideal that the term *Stewardship of Wellness* is derived.

Reconstruction

The need for rebuilding and making sense of a disaster or crisis psychologically starts the instant the amygdala of the brain sets into motion a person's survival mode. Over the first forty-eight to seventy-two hours, the senses take in what has unfolded, and the brain attempts to make sense of the chaos and trauma. The level of impact seen is dependent on many factors including past traumatic events, one's personality, resilience levels, and actual or perceived support systems available. This is similar to what happens with physical reconstruction, which does not start until after disaster struck, ended, and damage is assessed. All the while, a person's mind, body, and soul react to what's been experienced and are thrust into survival mode.

Because the threat to a person's cognitive, behavioral, emotional, psychological, and spiritual states of survival is aroused, many aftereffects can take place. This is why knowledgeable support is so important to overall wellbeing. People naturally assign meaning to the entire ordeal and the longer a detrimental understanding stays, the greater the risk of long-term compromise to wellness and one's mental health. *Stewardship of Mind* means gaining appreciation for and having the ability to maintain the wellness of our mind, which no one wants to lose. Compromised or strained mental health impacts the entire body. Have you ever been told by a doctor that the cause of some ailment is stress? A snapshot of the ways "body talk" manifests stress and is asking for help is provided as an appendix[7] for a more practical use and as a printable self-evaluating resource.

Additionally, reconstruction from a mental health perspective cannot take place without awareness of the attention that the body needs. That makes Stewardship of Wellness and Stewardship of Mind concepts worth exploring from the lens of scripture. Keeping a sober mind means more than just refraining from insobriety. Even sleep deprivation leads to the same impaired brain function as that of a drunk driver. A sober mind is a well mind.

THEOLOGICAL JUXTAPOSITION

This interesting similarity between scripture and the phases of disaster not only ignited the drive to publish this book, it will be a driving force in continued study of scripture to expand how we can lead more effectively in crisis ministry.

THREAT

The phasic parallels are as follows, and as this is presented, consider how the depravity of man factors into the scheme of the rise and decline of wellbeing—mind, body, and soul.

There existed in the garden an impending threat. The threat would bring consequences *only if* the warning was disregarded. This

---

7   See Appendix IV *How Trauma Stress Can Manifest: Body Talk That Is Asking For Help*. It is recommended or visible access following stressful or crisis incidents so the buddy system can look out for each other as well as spot early indicators of a need for self-care.

happens in storms all the time. Some plan, prepare, and respond to warnings, and others do not.

WARNING

Warnings serve to help us, not threaten us. We have free wills, and it seems most kind and loving that we know in advance what outcomes can result if we don't heed a warning, so that our choice is not made in ignorance. When we choose to counter the wisdom a warning provides, it compromises wellness, peace, and harmonious relationships.

God did not threaten Adam and Eve. God warned them about an existing threat. He did this so that free will would be exactly that—the freedom for individual choice. The threat was the outcome of eating a particular tree in the midst of the garden. Recovery and reconstruction were already part of the plan, provisionally proactive on God's part. The threat was a broken fellowship with God; a spiritual death or awakening, depending on how you choose to look at it. The power that comes with knowledge was the temptation.

The warning was that eating from the Tree of the Knowledge of Good and Evil would result in death. What sovereign grace God showed in keeping it simple: "You eat all else that is available, and you live. If you choose to eat from this one tree there is death." The knowledge that resulted from the choice made was mankind's ability to realize broken fellowship, fear, and corruption of the flesh that was made in the image of God, yet not like God in every way.

IMPACT

Eve ate. Then Adam succumbed to her poor example, and he ate too, and sin entered the world. Sin is the impactful event that causes us crisis. It is how all humanity enters the world and how the world currently exists. The phasic progression from impact to heroic, then honeymoon onto disillusionment is multifaceted and more complex than the linear phases we see in disasters. It requires a theological perspective and understanding of time, both eternal and chronological times as in epochs, historical and prophetic, and ecclesiology as well as eschatology. We will not get too deep in the weeds, but let's remember weeds are part of the curse resulting from the fall of man.

HEROIC

God so loved the world that He gave His only begotten Son to atone for sin, even before the foundations of the earth. He says through the book of Hebrews:

> *But about the Son he says,*
> *"Your throne, O God, will last for ever and ever; a scepter of justice will be the scepter of your kingdom. ⁹ You have loved righteousness and hated wickedness; therefore God, your God, has set you above your companions by anointing you with the oil of joy."*
>
> *¹⁰ He also says, "In the beginning, Lord, you laid the foundations of the earth, and the heavens are the work of your hands. ¹¹ They will perish, but you remain; they will all wear out like a garment. ¹² You will roll them up like a robe; like a garment they will be changed. But you remain the same, and your years will never end." ¹³ To which of the angels did God ever say, "Sit at my right hand until I make your enemies a footstool for your feet"?*
>
> *¹⁴ Are not all angels ministering spirits sent to serve those who will inherit salvation?*
> — Hebrews 1:8-14

This is where it is critical for the church to understand what may be held within returning members and visitors that seek spiritual guidance from the church.

Comparatively, similarities exist between Phasic Progressions of Disaster and the progression of the Bible—Genesis to Revelation. We have a threat, warning, and event leading up to the honeymoon phase whereby help and hope are fulfilled when Christ conquered the grave. Romans 5 is explicit in its detail of man's crisis and Jesus Christ as the savior and hero.

Given that the crucifixion was a traumatic event, found throughout the gospels are varied expressions of disillusionment from reactive behaviors of those present. We see the behaviors from the time of Jesus' arrest through the scattering of the disciples until the resurrected Christ appeared to them. The three days of uncertainty before He appeared to them after rising from the dead flow through the same complex pattern as disaster phases unfold.

Because of the resurrection and fulfillment of prophecy, man believed anew and those who had believed were affirmed in their faith. Now commissioned with purpose, they were impassioned to proclaim the good news. Here again is a shadowing image of the heroic message of hope that is now to be delivered to a world that remains threatened by spiritual death. The reconstruction phase then took the form of the early church. Today's church continues the recovery and anniversary phases, progressing toward the ultimate reconstruction of a new heaven and new earth after Christ's Second Coming.

No one knows exactly what the toll on overall wellness will be for mankind as the end of our world as we know it draws near. What we do know at this point is that there exist aversions to some crisis events and not to others. We also know that people in need of hope turn to those they assume can help them with spiritual support, and when that does not happen, the church as a whole is thought to have failed that person when they needed encouragement and the presence of Christ in their suffering.

STEWARDSHIP OF WELLNESS

For the very reason that leaders are held to a higher accountability, it is important to know how to minister to those who are trying to return to a form of normalcy. Prayer requests are the vehicle of one's crying out for help. Spiritual support in stress management and applied psychological first aid must happen. Many churches are large and volunteer-driven. Volunteers are the leaders engaged with through small groups or discipleship classes. It is at these intimate levels that people share vulnerabilities. While some form of Bible study is at the core of small group discipleship, ministry often takes direction as life unfolds in situations possibly not preached about or openly addressed by the church.

As leaders mentor and guide the flock, they are stewards of opportunities to love and serve others. If someone asks that you carry their load one mile, as a leader, you must follow the principle to go the extra mile to serve them well. It is one thing to discuss mental health as having a stigma that must end. It is a completely different matter to have the conversation and equip leaders to recognize signs of declining wellness when one is going through divorce, abandonment, loss of jobs, etc. People do not arrive at a palace of desperation, such as self-harm, without exhibiting some indication. Prevention is stewarding the sanctity of life. There are far too many that have experienced the impact of the moral injury which is so hard for church leaders to face.

Giving brotherly love means we love and are available, even in the worst of times. When we get better at mitigating on the front end of catastrophes, we mitigate the one thing so difficult to do: break the silence about suicide.

RECOVERY

The recovery phase of disasters and the casualty rates deserve attention beyond the mental health field. For the very reason that many people turn to the church, it is imperative such leaders be aware of the following and are equipped to serve. For reasons of residual impact and potential compromise to overall health after traumatic stress events, the church has an opportunity to step into a significant role in spiritual support in recovery.

The footprint of anguish in any disaster will always be much larger than the medical footprint, with the mental health of four to fifty times more casualties impacted. This is particularly true in a situation such as the pandemic our world currently faces. What exists is the potential for far greater numbers of those impacted who carry invisible wounds and individuals with lived experience.

"In the wake of pandemic and other critical incidents there is invariably an increased demand for spiritual and psychological support due to an increased acute distress and dysfunction referred to as surge." Empirical evidence estimates that 20 to 40% of the directly affected population could prosper from some form of social emotional and spiritual support, including CISM intervention, and or psychological/spiritual first aid, be it in small group interactive interventions or as one to one debriefing conversations. Such skills are much-needed among church vocational and volunteer leaders.[8]

The COVID pandemic in its longevity means that the church will likely be faced with more needs to minister to than it is prepared to skillfully provide. We are not yet in a reconstruction phase in this crisis.

Past situations of similar nature that impacted jobs and the economy at a similar level include the Spanish flu of 1918. Quarantines and social distancing worked to save lives. At the same time, such lifesaving measures eroded human resilience. Another crisis, The Great Depression, resulted in many suicides. Our current situation is already faced with a change in mortality rates caused by suicide at alarming numbers for ages ten to upwards of eight-five, according The World Health Organization. With suicide being the second leading cause of death in students fifteen to twenty-four today, we must not only pay attention to the times, proactive measures must be implemented in order to serve others accordingly. While the world is not easy, we are talking about preventable deaths, and the earlier the mitigation, the greater the possibility of saving lives physically as well as spiritually.

---

8   Psychological First Aid (PFA) When Disaster Strikes.

SOCIAL DISTANCE

How has social distancing impacted you? Not only is the term "social distancing" an oxymoron, but it also challenges human nature because we are designed for fellowship and to love one another. Proximity and interaction are most beneficial when socializing includes the healthy non-verbal communication of human touch, even if only a fist bump, high-five, or pat on the back. What concerns me as a responder and crisis mitigator is that anything less than regular and not less than eight appropriate contacts leads to deprivation. No digital platform can substitute for man's hunger for love.

Historically casualties of emotional injury following disasters surface weeks, months, and years after the event. Because emotional or psychological injury impacts mental health and that many people will turn to friends, coworkers, and clergy before considering a mental health professional, growth and development for all people are needed. Neglect or resistance to change is sin. Hope deferred when those seeking help encounter more than disappointment during times of spiritual vulnerability. Proverbs 13:12 is clear that the result is a sick heart.

On some level, disasters are inevitable, be they personal, familial, natural, or man-made catastrophe. How one navigates and communicates Christ through them involves a series of choices with the options limited by what we do not know and the available skills we can activate in the hour of need. How one responds may not change the entire world, but it will impact the world and lives of those ministered to, and it will develop the one called upon to minister. For this reason, evaluations after events about what worked, what needs improvement, and lessons learned contribute to growth and effectiveness. It is pertinent to this discussion to focus on how God calls His people to be prepared to give an answer for what they believe. This principle is not limited to an apologetic response in conversation. The words of 1 Peter 3:14-16 are directives of how to live, to respond versus to react. We will elaborate on "response versus reaction" later. When situations are beyond control, yet foreseeable, is it not in our ability and perhaps our responsibility to act according to the sanctity of life?

While grace and encouragement are often present for others, they are often deficiently applied personally by ministers who have a hard inner-critic. Self-assessment of how a situation transpired and one's personal role is evaluated in reflection. At that point, one will either be reconciled with one's actions or will become spiritually vulnerable if second-guessing, doubt, or guilt crash into the aftermath. In preparing this chapter, many pastors and leaders of pastors were interviewed to provide useful content.

A few things that came to light are the insights of personal impact and the need to pastor differently, as well as the importance of presence in mental health. From introvert to extrovert, the common theme was how hard it is to be called to love and love on people and not be able to even be with them. Is it any wonder that church leaders also succumb to discouragement, anxiety, depression, or various forms of compromised mental health just like anyone else? Ministers are humans as are responders. They can become fatigued by compassion or an empathetic sense of obligation or pride-driven need to be all things to all men so that some may be saved. It is not humanly possible. No one else is the apostle Paul, and the demands of contemporary times differ from those of the first century. The topics of need and the importance of self-care recurred in the majority of those I interviewed, while few had a pre-existing plan on managing personal stress.

The expectations imposed on ministers and ironically at times embraced by them to meet all needs is unreasonable. Christ works through His body, the church, utilizing each member of the whole, including the global parts. Grace and mercy are attributes it behooves every minister to exercise on the "inner critic." Words have the power of life and death. Words aptly spoken, especially the dialogue of self-talk, either align with truths that are believed, or create inner and unseen conflict as a result of the lies personally believed. All are vulnerable, and no believer is exempt from maturation and learning. The cost of not doing so is far greater than when we consider a compromise in the *Stewardship of Wellness*. The cost is the precious lives at stake.

PRESENCE

It should come as no surprise that when individuals face a crisis, spiritual leaders, peers, and mentors will be turned to for help. As a leader, are you ready? This is not a time for inquiry or opinion. People reach out in hopes of being met with compassion and love, and many times it is silence and presence without judgment that the one in need is seeking. The testimony of someone's presence affirms faith and hope in a person in crisis. It is imperative to have the discernment that occasionally, when we seek to fill the thick airwaves of a person's lowest point with powerful truths, we may do more harm than good. Speaking the truth in love must consider that truths from the perspective of one not deeply impacted can hit a hurting soul. The enemy will make your words sound like false religious platitudes that can twist and escalate the crisis beyond an outcry made for care. The enemy's method of operation as a liar and accuser uses the skin of truth to make the lies palatable.[9] Needs in an emergency may include words of hope, referral to other community resources, or something more tangible, such as food, temporary shelter, or other needs so that a person can move beyond survival. The aftermath of a crisis must lead to stability. It is mission-critical that spiritual support and follow-up happen. Gone must be the days of doing ministry around stigma and tiptoeing around subjects that have been taboo. Silence is detrimental. Presence is not. A ministry of presence validates personal significance. Consequently, the absence of presence or perceived dismissal of care sends a conflicting message easily misinterpreted by a wounded soul. The enemy loves to fuel feelings and feed thoughts so that

---

9   Revelation 12:10 *"...for the accuser of our brethren has been thrown down, he who accuses them before our God day and night."* This has been ongoing since the fall of man and it continues until the inception of the new heaven and earth..

wrong thinking leads to embracing lies that over time become beliefs. A person may or may not feel they are important to the church as a whole, and that lie has resulted in the walking wounded: those that leave church altogether or abandon fellowship when it is most needed.

At a time in history when preventable deaths are an escalating threat and among them are deaths by suicides in children, the church must muster courage. The World Health Organization is well aware that "Suicides and suicide attempts have a ripple effect that impacts on families, friends, colleagues, communities and societies. Suicides are preventable. Much can be done to prevent suicide at individual, community and national levels." I firmly believe that now is the time to better learn how to serve one another further concerning crisis ministry.

Transformation by renewing the minds of leaders about how to recognize our role as a church in eschatology starts now. There exists a very large population impacted, yet not experiencing the kind of ministry that lends to healing and breaking through the lies believed. The enemy will continue to use fear and concern of liability to prevent a ministry of presence and even more so to maintain the absence of teaching restorative living. To improve, we must be willing to ask questions and be prepared to listen to better gain understanding of what may not be known because of our avoidance. We must gain compassion by replacing ignorance with unheard perspectives. Suicide prevention needs to start at the onset of trauma stress following tragic incidents.

The application is to equip yourself. Brainstorm with others about how to collaborate to form a ministry that meets these needs. Mentor one another, ask questions of those with insight in areas in which you are lacking! Be strong and courageous, do not fear what man can do, revere what the Lord will do in and through you. Yes, you.

The awareness of biblical theology, held beliefs, with a willingness to grow and become most effective in even the most uncomfortable situations, are the catalyst for growth and improvement. Through biblical guidance and contextual use of historical evidence that aligns with scripture and trends concerning the human condition (1 Timothy 4), we have an excellent opportunity to grow. Spiritual maturity and ministry development and improvement are the results of awareness and growth. For that reason, a continuous progression through the considerations of divinity within diversity must be looked at in general and precisely how the aftermath times of crisis are indicative of rudimentary problems. As the foundation builds, it will lead us to how all these factors make a compelling case toward the Stewardship of Wellness and Stewardship of Mind concepts. Moving forward, we transition to the topic of diversity into the mystery of the unknown and to discover how we might love one another more like Christ.

DIVINE DIVERSITY

Then Peter began to speak: "I now realize how true it is that God does not show favoritism but accepts from every nation the one who fears him and does what is right. You know the message God sent to the people of Israel, announcing the good news of peace through Jesus Christ, who is Lord of all."

— Acts 10:34-36

SENSITIVITY WARNING

L anguage within this contextual story is used only to demonstrate the innocence and ignorance of children. The reader's reaction and thoughts can provide priceless personal insight. No slander, malice, or ill-intent is intended, moreover, the author does not condone prejudice or racism of any kind. Grace, mercy, and forgiveness are asked for in advance.

The problem of living in a world impacted by the crisis of sin, while waiting for the hope of Christ's return, is seen in the conflicts we create. Elitism and racism are not eternal, nor are they God-glorifying. They were introduced to human nature when sin entered the heart of man. There is no racism in heaven, and as such, racism has no place on earth, where we are called to live according to God's Kingdom-principles. While many will argue that the Bible is discriminatory, racism truly has no place in our lives. What has become a point of great division is how to act when a person chooses to live contrary to what is biblical. The world's demands and expectations that we show tolerance and acceptance of unbiblical lifestyles by adapting them as if they are biblical is creating immense conflict within believers and between believers and others. The tension is between knowing how to love a person and still call that which is sin, sin! Sin is ungodly; it is judged by God and poses a struggle for Christians. How do we reconcile attitudes with Christ like behavior that is not misinterpreted to be hateful of another? The late pastor W. A. Criswell once said, "A skunk by any other name is still a skunk!"

Perceived discrimination may not be meant to be against an individual person. The problem is that when people are hurt, they do not communicate well. Words, behaviors, silence, and estrangements all convey something, and more often than not, what is meant is not how the recipient interprets what was said or done. Becoming more like Christ does result in tensions between the lost and the redeemed. Being transformed is a divine process that challenges the believer and an unbelieving world of how to rightly maintain a constant witness that glorifies God for advancing the gospel. Everyone deals with pride and prejudice. To deny it is an outright lie. What many perceive as discrimination concerning sin is a lack of understanding of how to best express God's love, ministering to sinners just as Christ did, while at the same time not condoning sin. We see the question of how to love one another as being open to interpretation, yet scripture is not silent on the matter.

Consider this story. A little girl went to kindergarten, excited and eager to learn. She noticed that each student was unique. Before then, most of the children she had spent time with were family, except for one neighbor from Istanbul. One thing caught her attention in a particular way as she made friends. Another little girl shared her name and then said, "I am Mexican."

After school, she was eager to tell her dad all about the day. In great detail, she shared her story, including how many Mexicans were in her class. She was quite impressed that several had the same last name, and like where she had lived before, several were cousins. To her confusion, he disagreed and claimed there was one more

Mexican in the class than she counted. She gave him names again, counted, and still there were only five. He sent her to the mirror three times, instructing her to search it for another Mexican. She insisted she did not see another Mexican in the mirror; it was only her. Then he walked her to the mirror and stood behind her. He pointed into the reflection and told her to look closely. Then he asked what she saw. Innocently she said she only saw herself and him. He told her to look carefully and she would see a Mexican. She peered into the mirror, quite confused. Looking at her reflection, then at his reflection, she searched the entire mirror, looking for the Mexican her dad told her that she would see. Nothing. Suddenly she noticed something. Her dad's reflection reminded her of one of the boy's coloring. She looked down at her hand next to his on the dresser. Her skin was much lighter. He turned her chin back to the mirror and asked if she had found the Mexican yet? Turning back to look at him with uncertainty and hesitancy, she wondered if he was a Mexican. To her shock, his reply was, "Yes." He went on to explain that if he was Mexican, then so was she. The little girl was confused. This event started an identity crisis for that young girl.

Hearing frequent name-calling that included the use of derogatory language otherwise unknown to the girl, she too occasionally used some of the words she heard from adults around her. She knew no differently. The earlier incident of discovering her heritage prompted questioning her identity. She dealt with many doubts and often questioned the validity of who she was and how to think of others. She often sought confirmation. She was a sensitive and perceptive child, with a keen sense of right and wrong. She loved people and loved to learn. One day while riding her bike, she saw a dark man walking on the sidewalk and felt discouraged that she could not go past someone blocking the path. She thought back to a time when her dad had used a word to refer to a man who looked like him. She boldly and with great curiosity, rode up to the man in her path and asked if indeed he was a "meager." Although that was what was said, something felt within her felt very uncomfortable after she asked the man her question. Again, she asked, but more cautiously. His facial expression stirred a sadness in her. He stared at the girl for a moment and then replied. His response sent her back so excited to tell her dad about the great discovery. She rode back toward her dad, shouting, "Daddy! I just talked to a …" Dad laughed and swept her into his arms. Then she noticed glances exchanged between the man and her dad. That bothered her and left her with a sense that something was wrong.

Innocent and naive, she did what was instructed. She had no idea that the use of such a word was derogatory, hurtful, and inappropriate. That little girl later learned the pain of racism when someone called her a "beaner" and referred to her as a "stupid Mexican." Crushed and with a fairer complexion like her mother, who was of Irish and Spanish descent, she felt the need to deny the newfound identity. She had concluded that if she was a Mexican and no one had told her before going to school, it must have been a secret from her because there was something wrong with it. In her mind, if she was Mexican, then why wasn't she included or counted among those classmates at school? They seemed grouped by the teachers and they stuck together all the time.

Her notice of inconsistencies came naturally. She experienced kids in the neighborhood who asked if they could touch her skin and who asked what it felt like to be a Mexican. That little girl struggled much of her life, questioning her identity. She often struggled to answer when asked what her heritage was. How is this relevant? That little girl was me. Perhaps there are things about my story that resonate with how you've learned behaviors and attitudes that either show love or hate. I challenge you to surrender every hesitance and resistance to love others. Allow God to address the heart issue that is racism.

Children learn from influencers very much like a sponge, absorbing all kinds of vocabulary, attitudes, behaviors, and habits. Adults also adapt to influencers. Adults allow others to make a lasting impression on us. At some point, we assess how the influencers contribute to who we become while at other times, there is intentionally choosing who we want to influence us. What, if any, form of racism did you learn early in life? The story was told in the third person because that was me *before* I turned to Christ and He transformed my life. He continues to do so, as I am an eager disciple. The complexity of growing up questioning my identity included vehemently pursuing answers as to why so many family members were part of the Buffalo Regiment during the Civil War. When I learned that my great-grandfather was a black man, many things became clear. The years following brought awareness of how that had impacted my father and uncles who, being orphaned, grew up in a very small, segregated town. What matters today is who I am because of Christ and how much He changes everything.

For application in how to let God do in you what He desires concerning unity, prayerfully seek Him so that every form of racism is transformed to brotherly love. Such a challenge is in order to have God search our hearts about how we live in or conflicted by the truth. Truth is not a perception, opinion, or mere fact, absolute truth trumps facts and sets captives free.

Consider the behavior of lying.

> *Do not lie to each other, since you have taken off your old self with its practices* ¹⁰ *and have put on the new self, which is being renewed in knowledge in the image of its Creator.* ¹¹ *Here there is no Gentile or Jew, circumcised or uncircumcised, barbarian, Scythian, slave or free, but Christ is all, and is in all.*
>
> ¹² *Therefore, as God's chosen people, holy and dearly loved, clothe yourselves with compassion, kindness, humility, gentleness and patience.* ¹³ *Bear with each other and forgive one another if any of you has a grievance against someone. Forgive as the Lord forgave you.* ¹⁴ *And over all these virtues put on love, which binds them all together in perfect unity.*
>
> — Colossians 3: 9-14

If speaking lies to others is unacceptable, then how much more unacceptable are the lies that we hold on to or that are rooted in misguided beliefs? This discipline should stir us spiritually to consider if the church to which we are an actual witness is more like

Christ's bride or the church at Laodicea.[10] God forbid the opposition of an unbelieving world, that continues to gradually come against religious liberties and professing faith in Christ, has resulted in lukewarm Christianity. We must repent of complacency.

COMPLACENCY

Complacency has no place in the life of a Christian. Its presence is an opportunity for God to do a triumphant work in us. The Bible confronts the topic with stern and timeless warnings. God created the world, yet it is populated by sinful men, many of whom live without regard to who God is. That is the status quo. He loves and desires a personal relationship with everyone, anyway. However, that is a relationship He will not force. Each person must choose to follow Jesus Christ as Lord, Savior, and Sovereign. The decline of monarchy rulers has resulted in the unfamiliarity in our western culture of what a "sovereign" is.

As a leader, Vince Lombardi started each football season with his NFL players the same way. Holding up the pointed oval pigskin ball, he declared it to be a "football." The men were professional athletes. They knew this truth already. However, yearly he explained the importance of knowing how to handle the basic tools of the game. Even with championship-winning teams, the principles of the basics were reset in everyone's mind and heart each season. The number of victories did not matter. What mattered was mentorship.

Christianity has a resource far more excellent with stakes higher than any championship this world has to offer: the Bible. The intentional application of what scripture teaches must be a top-of-mind discipline to Christian living. So that by it, each member who makes up the church *is* the body of Christ, not merely part of a congregation of spiritual consumers. We must be subject to and adoring to sovereign rule. In the case of Christ, sovereignty is

---

10 Revelation 3:15-16 15 *"I know your deeds, that you are neither cold nor hot. I wish you were either one or the other! 16 So, because you are lukewarm— neither hot nor cold—I am about to spit you out of my mouth."*

not limited to inheritance. It originates eternally because He is the King of Kings. He is the only king ever capable of so great a love that He traded places with every soul on the cross so that justice would be settled and righteousness would be available for all who desire forgiveness.

Racism has no place in the Kingdom of God. It is contrary to the throne room scenes found in Revelation:

> *And they sang a new song, saying: "You are worthy to take the scroll and to open its seals, because you were slain, and with your blood you purchased for God persons from every tribe and language and people and nation.*
>
> — Revelation 5:59

Scripture is clear about unity. It is time individuals bend the knee before God, and let transformation start individually. Individually, one person cannot change the world, but the world of each individual changing as result of submitting to God as Sovereign *will* change the world.

> *After this I looked, and there before me was a great multitude that no one could count, from every nation, tribe, people and language, standing before the throne and before the Lamb. They were wearing white robes and were holding palm branches in their hands.*
>
> — Revelation 7:9

Racism also goes against what the Apostle Paul taught.

> *Here there is no Gentile or Jew, circumcised or uncircumcised, barbarian, Scythian, slave or free, but Christ is all, and is in all.*
>
> — Colossians 3:11

In the following sections, the prominence of scripture and what it challenges the reader to consider is essential. I pray that a spiritual self-examination would lead to a transformational surge that revives a resurrected passion a thousand times more than the day you surrendered to Christ!

Test yourself according to God's word.

> *Examine yourselves to see whether you are in the faith; test yourselves. Do you not realize that Christ Jesus is in you—unless, of course, you fail the test?*
>
> — 2 Corinthians 13:5

Failure is not final; moreover, it is a merciful opportunity to humbly confess to the Lord how reliant we must be on Him. Subsequently, what follows is the process to be transformed by the renewing of our minds. A solid understanding of the importance of any discipline compels motivation to pursue such a goal. A look at the warnings against this and a few reasons we ought to ask the Lord for transformation is in order.

RISKS AND WARNINGS

> *Do not conform to the pattern of this world, but be transformed by the renewing of your mind. Then you will be able to test and approve what God's will is—his good, pleasing and perfect will.*
>
> — Romans 12:2

> *No discipline seems pleasant at the time, but painful. Later on, however, it produces a harvest of righteousness and peace for those who have been trained by it.*
>
> — Hebrews 12:11

Is complacency present in these verses? Consider the options and choose this day whom you will serve. Growth and learning require unlearning and destroying practices, habits, or patterns that have become unused structures that occupy space on the foundation of our beliefs.

> *The high places, however, were not removed, and the people still had not set their hearts on the God of their ancestors.*
>
> — 2 Chronicles 20:33

While it may be uncomfortable to consider, we must allow God to have authority in everything about us—even what we have not yet discovered. We do have options, but keep in mind that either we choose volitionally or by apathy. I pray the best choices are made.

BIBLICAL CONSIDERATIONS

In his pride the wicked man does not seek him; in all his thoughts there is no room for God.

— Psalm 10:4

My people come to you, as they usually do, and sit before you to hear your words, but they do not put them into practice. Their mouths speak of love, but their hearts are greedy for unjust gain.

— Ezekiel 33:31

We do not want you to become lazy, but to imitate those who through faith and patience inherit what has been promised.

— Hebrews 6:12

See to it that you do not refuse him who speaks. If they did not escape when they refused him who warned them on earth, how much less will we, if we turn away from him who warns us from heaven?

— Hebrews 12:25

EXAMPLES

There are many examples of various manners of smug living with satisfaction apart from God. Let us not go the way of destructive living. The context of scripture must always be considered historically and as applicable for the believer. All scripture is timeless and for present active and ongoing growth.

> *This is the way of an adulterous woman: She eats and wipes her mouth and says, 'I've done nothing wrong.'*
>
> — Proverbs 30:20

> *"Son of man, say to the ruler of Tyre, 'This is what the Sovereign Lord says: "'In the pride of your heart you say, "I am a god; I sit on the throne of a god in the heart of the seas." But you are a mere mortal and not a god, though you think you are as wise as a god.*
>
> — Ezekiel 28:2

We must realize that we are the temple of the living God.[11] Many people live as if procrastination and intended desires to do or complete something is in our control.[12] Time is in God's hands, and when we hear the Spirit call; we need to take action immediately.[13]

> *This is what the Lord Almighty says: "These people say, 'The time has not yet come to rebuild the Lord's house.'"*
>
> — Haggai 1:2

> *But everyone who hears these words of mine and does not put them into practice is like a foolish man who built his house on sand.*
>
> — Matthew 7:26

These examples are not exhaustive of how much scripture has to say to encourage a return to our Creator. God knows man wants to go in his own way, and ultimately, it is a personal choice, but God is clear that He wants a return to Him. It is better to commit than to give any excuse.

---

11 2 Corinthians 6:16 *What agreement is there between the temple of God and idols? For we are the temple of the living God. As God has said: "I will live with them and walk among them, and I will be their God, and they will be my people."*

12 James 4:14 *Why, you do not even know what will happen tomorrow. What is your life? You are a mist that appears for a little while and then vanishes.*

13 Hebrews 3:15 *As has just been said: "Today, if you hear his voice, do not harden your hearts as you did in the rebellion."*

> *"But they all alike began to make excuses. The first said, 'I have just bought a field, and I must go and see it. Please excuse me.'"*
>
> — Luke 14:18

God's mercy and grace when it comes to His justice is why He has given us full disclosure of what will result when we do not personally consider where we each stand in our relationship to the Lord God Almighty. Stick through this chapter; just ahead, there is encouraging news!

PROPOSED RESPONSE

What if each believer in Christ committed to pray through the following conviction as a soul-searching prayer? If we sought the Lord to reveal obstacles, what would prevent a commitment to live according to the following statement of conviction? Would you commit to lead by example in this way?

COMMITMENT OF CONVICTION

As a believer, Christ-follower, and leader within the church, I declare a unified and immovable stance that racism or racial discrimination in any form is sinful and will not be overlooked or tolerated in our churches or community.

In this public declaration, we stand together that racism, whether explicit or implicit, is incompatible with the teaching of our Lord Jesus. It was Jesus who elevated the commandment, "Love your neighbor as yourself" to the prominence given to "Love the Lord your God with all your heart and with all your soul and with all your mind" (Matthew 22:37-39).

Recognizing silence makes us complicit. We, the church, have been silent for far too long. We unapologetically declare that any racist attitude or action is sinful and runs contrary to what God requires. We must respond with confession and, in turn, rejection of racism and discrimination throughout the congregation. We will serve as a voice of love and biblical justice for all who are oppressed, mistreated, and disregarded.

We affirm every member of our community regardless of race or ethnicity and welcome each to our community as our neighbors. We pledge to you that our city will be a city of inclusion and hospitality to all.

Driven by our faith in the Lord Jesus, we implore every member of our respective churches to stand with us in our determination to see the sin of racism come to an end in our community. Together, we will embrace the Prophet Micah's challenge "to act justly and to love mercy and to walk humbly with your God" (Micah 6:8).

BENEFITS AND PROMISES

God loves you. There are circumstances that He allows and others that we choose that lead to the outcomes in our lives and the world around us. Although many only focus on the positive, kind, and loving attributes of the Lord, it is good news for us that He is righteous and holy. We must also embrace that, just as any loving father does, God disciplines those He loves.

> *Moreover, we have all had human fathers who disciplined us and we respected them for it. How much more should we submit to the Father of spirits and live!* [10] *They disciplined us for a little while as they thought best; but God disciplines us for our good, in order that we may share in his holiness.* [11] *No discipline seems pleasant at the time, but painful. Later on, however, it produces a harvest of righteousness and peace for those who have been trained by it.*
> — Hebrews 12:9-11

In His mercy and grace, through all things, there is hope. The promises that follow impart the benefits of living according to God's plan. Blessings abound.

Knowledge

Your informed decisions lead to a higher possibility that you will embrace the hope available through God's promises. Isaiah 58 has a profound lesson for us all. God's people had prayed and fasting amiss when the Lord clarified His desire, so that His promises and blessing could be released.

> *Is not this the kind of fasting I have chosen: to loose the chains of injustice and untie the cords of the yoke, to set the oppressed free and break every yoke?*
> *7 Is it not to share your food with the hungry and to provide the poor wanderer with shelter—when you see the naked, to clothe them, and not to turn away from your own flesh and blood?*
> — Isaiah 58:6-7

When submission happens, God's promises and blessings pour forth—subsequently impacting individuals and the world. God's people have a responsibility as a "when then" or "if-then" beneficiary of God answering prayer, as found in 2 Chronicles 7:14.[14] We must be mindful and consider our heart attitudes and behaviors, especially about prejudice, hate, and racism. When a man does what he ought, then God responds as He promised. He is not restricted; we, who are called to be holy yet by ungodly living, prohibit what is reserved for righteous people.

The following list of blessings come as a result of how we love God through loving one another.

Fourteen Promises

These promises are taken directly from Isaiah 58:9-14

- "The Lord will answer in this way, according to His promise…"
- Your light will rise in the darkness
- Your night will become like the noonday.

---

14 *"If my people, who are called by my name, will humble themselves and pray and seek my face and turn from their wicked ways, then I will hear from heaven, and I will forgive their sin and will heal their land."*

- The Lord will guide you always;
- The Lord will satisfy your needs
- The Lord will strengthen your frame.
- You will be like a well-watered garden,
- Your people will rebuild the ancient ruins
- Your people will raise up the age-old foundations;
- You will be called Repairer of Broken Walls, Restorer of Streets with Dwellings.
- You will find your joy in the Lord,
- God will cause you to ride in triumph
- God will cause you to feast on the inheritance of your father Jacob."
- You need to take my word for it.

Isaiah 58:14 "For the mouth of the Lord has spoken."

PERSONAL APPLICATION

Before moving ahead in reading, Consider the next few questions as you give yourself a pause to ask the Holy Spirit to reveal what prohibits your ability to love others as He loves you.

Now consider someone standing in front of you. What prevents a willingness to walk a week in the shoes of that person? What fears or concerns keep you from a resounding, yes?

Pivotal encounters with others are inevitable and most likely surround you every day. Too often, we critique the church for failures in these encounters. But how often have we individually cried out for transformation in the world to start with us, personally? When was the last time you asked a question and then listened with intentionality? When has that intention to listen overridden the temptation to let that conversation slip by as casual, when it had the opportunity to be so much more? Listen with the purpose of gaining insight as to how you can love and serve others better. In the previous chapter, attention was given to the power and importance of asking questions as a ministry strategy. Ask someone, "What do you wish someone would ask you?" Armed with the surety that you want to hear the answers, knowing you may not like them, you can brace yourself for truths that will be helpful to implementing change. Prepare in advance how you plan to respond when an answer is brutally honest and may stir opposing sentiments. This is an introductory lesson in how personal crisis arises and how, as stewards, we must learn to spiritually manage stressors in life that are truly opportunities to glorify God.

It can be convicting to consider the challenges presented so far, but do believe that what the Lord desires by his command that we love one another is that we do so well. Diversity exists for a reason and with a purpose, we must grow as a result of it. As we turn attention to the topic of stewardship different from that of finances, let us bear in mind that even our breath is a gift given and operating every molecule of our being, which makes up God's temple for believers. Maintenance is not optional; it is necessary. Wellness is something we all want. Generally, people do not long to be ill at any level. Stewardship of Wellness is not a new concept, but it needs explaining so that the content ahead remains relevant personally. The next three sections of this comprehensive introduction, I pray, will bring you to a place of appreciation for what you have. You have a life that is a gift. You have repeated opportunities even in this book to hear what the Holy Spirit may be saying through scripture. Moreover, you have every opportunity to make a difference. Stewardship of Wellness will lead to discovering mysteries unknown and then how powerful the hindsight of testimony is in the Kingdom of God's economy.

STEWARDSHIP OF WELLNESS

K nowing that your body is the temple of the Living God, stewardship of all that makes up who you are is nothing to take lightly. This includes your health. "Health" encompasses more than the absence of illness. Wellbeing includes a fit mind, body, and soul. When scripture instructs that the Word of God brings strength to your body and nourishment to your bones and that you should taste and know that it is good, you need to know these phrases are more than mere metaphor. The absorbing and soul-penetrating ability of God's Word to transform your life is meant for the wellness of all that is mental, emotional, physical, psychological, spiritual, and behavioral. So how much value and stewardship do you place on your health and wellness?

Is the church equipping towards the return of Christ where wellness is concerned? Has she kept pace with, fallen behind, or led the way in discussions of overall health from a stewardship aspect? Or has she, like much of the world, been reactive and selective about certain topics, some that include the stigma of moral injury and hard-to-reconcile travesties surrounding mental health? Discussions should not be limited to or predominantly address mental health gone awry. Given that scripture tells us to have a sound, sober mind of self-control, the church must consider what can be done to serve better when the aftermath of high stress or traumatic incidents impact the lives of so many people.

The *Stewardship of Wellness* is a Christocentric strategic approach to help people realize that each mind, body, and soul has value and benefit. Does the church teach and disciple about how

fearfully and wonderfully we are created? Does the church appreciate how sustained and maintained health glorifies God? Candidly
speaking, we all have mental health, the question is, how well have
we learned to maintain one of our most priceless assets: the mind?
Have members of the church discipled the vital principles of stewarding the mind and its wellbeing as a form of spiritual mental
health?

WELLNESS

I never fathomed that I might find myself in a situation where
verses like "we take captive every thought to make it obedient to
Christ" and "be transformed by the renewing of the mind" beck-
oned me in a desperate pursuit to live to honor God with voracious
conviction amid a personal tragedy. It sadly occurred to me through
my experience that not once in my many years in the church, catechism, Sunday school, small group discipleship, Bible study, Bible
college, or seminary attendance had anyone ever discussed *how* to
do these commands. To my recollection, no one had ever taught
"how to" do that which contributes to preventing the compromise
of one's health. It was a directive only touched on as something that
should be done. My soul begged for answers to the question: *How*
do I become transformed, when I do not know how to renew the
brokenness of a mind? My mind had succumbed to a low place and
no one had showed up to love me through to a better place. Praise
the Lord that He never leaves or forsakes us.

The world's message surrounding personal development is that
a person can reinvent himself (or herself) and that a person is the
"master" of his destiny. This creates in us a compelling pull to do
more in our own strength than we are meant to do apart from
the Holy Spirit's help, counsel, and guidance. God has a plan and
purpose best for you and uniquely for you. And you have a helper!
If we think *we* can reinvent what God created is to imply that we
can repurpose or recycle what could not otherwise be used by the
original owner. Co-creating is a completely different matter.

So what did I do in the aftermath of my crisis? I pursued answers to both of those "how" questions. My heart's desire was to grow according to the progression laid out in 2 Peter 1, and my pursuit was motivated by this promise:

> *Grace and peace be multiplied to you in the knowledge of God and of Jesus our Lord; 3 seeing that His divine power has granted to us everything pertaining to life and godliness, through the true knowledge of Him who called us by His own glory and excellence. 4 For by these He has granted to us His precious and magnificent promises, so that by them you may become partakers of the divine nature, having escaped the corruption that is in the world by lust. 5 Now for this very reason also, applying all diligence, in your faith supply moral excellence, and in your moral excellence, knowledge, 6 and in your knowledge, self-control, and in your self-control, perseverance, and in your perseverance, godliness, 7 and in your godliness, brotherly kindness, and in your brotherly kindness, love. 8 For if these qualities are yours and are increasing, they render you neither useless nor unfruitful in the true knowledge of our Lord Jesus Christ.*
>
> — 2 Peter 1:2-8

There was nothing small or complacent about the pursuit. I was fully aware that during a severe crisis I was in the crosshairs of the enemy. Were it not for the grace of Almighty God, I would not be alive to storm the gates of hell, part of which includes writing this book about what I learned. Teaching and equipping others with hope and working within the area of crisis management was part of His purpose for my life. God never wastes a hurt nor leaves a wound unattended. It is our neglect that misses out on growth and healing.

The world promotes the message that the pursuit of success must start with "why." However, scripture teaches not to ask why or lean on our own understanding, but to seek the Lord and He will direct our paths. Furthermore, He shows us great and mighty things we do not know, and all because He loves deeply. He is sovereign. When we ask, seek, and knock at wisdom's door, indeed the Holy Spirit counsels and helps beyond what is asked for or imagined. Not only does He provide direction, He ushers us into the blueprint designed for more than the world's definition of success. His leading results in flourishing and prospering according to the unique plan and purpose He has for each one of His treasured people.[15] Submission to a sovereign Lord is beautiful. Stewardship is caring for what God has entrusted to our care, acknowledging that it belongs fully to Him. It is more than giving a tithe. It includes all things.

MIND

Stewardship of Mind is grasping what it is to fix our eyes on Jesus. The eyes of the body are one thing, the vision within that a soul sees can only happen from the Lord's revelation and insight, according to the Scripture. His ways are not our ways, nor are our ways His ways. His perspective is not our perspective. We are, however, designed with a mind capable of growth, healing, transformation, and renewal. Alignment with Him is the key to allowing Him to accomplish those outcomes in us. Why this is not taught in church, I have no idea. We lack discipleship in some vital areas of Christian living.

When we have an enemy with a predictable method of operation, always lying and accusing, the thoughts he presents often become beliefs. The enemy is effective in his mission. His goals are the same every time; he seeks to kill in many ways concerning your spirit, hope, relationships, confidence, and esteem. He steals the identities forfeited by weary souls who have been wounded by the careless words of others. He destroys the human spirit, rendering

---

15 Deuteronomy 26:17-19 [17] *"You have today declared the Lord to be your God, and that you would walk in His ways and keep His statutes, His commandments and His ordinances, and listen to His voice.* [18] *The Lord has today declared you to be His people, a treasured possession, as He promised you, and that you should keep all His commandments;* [19] *and that He will set you high above all nations which He has made, for praise, fame, and honor; and that you shall be a consecrated people to the Lord your God, as He has spoken."*

some fearful, anxious, doubtful, and unbelieving of who the child of God truly is in Christ.

If only we could grasp that the eyes of our body are sensory. They communicate at speeds of intake beyond what is measurable. The words we speak and hear are also sensory and also quickly impact the brain. The brain, being the tangible storehouse of what enters the mind, processes the thoughts and ideas that either woo or wound our souls.

The human mind is worthy of stewardship. For through it we are transformed, renewed, and we maintain sobriety. It is by the authority of the blood of the lamb and the word of our testimony that one chooses to apply the word of God, so that the spiritual fruit of self-control is responsive and does not succumb to reactive living based on emotions or held captive by trauma. To live reactively on the whim of emotions is to become weary, heavily burdened, and in need of rest, which detrimentally means the enemy has ample opportunity to manipulate an unsuspecting soul. In these moments he manipulates us to think, act, and hold beliefs contrary to what is true and God-honoring. Emotions are a gift from our creator and are designed for experiential, memorable, and mind-alerting indicators. Emotions are also designed to signal discernment. When we do not test the spirits, one is open to making poor choices. It happens to believers and unbelievers alike. The mind submitted to Christ is sober, clear, and acts with the Spirit of God in control.

In my darkest hour, I may have acted contrary to anything I fully believed, but with all transparency, today I am well aware of the lies and how palatably they were ingested. Lies toxified my mind, then my body, and subsequently my soul sustained a moral injury that was self-caused and only God was capable of healing me. No amount of human counseling apart from God's work in and through me could have produced what is now a relentless servant. Only with my openness for His work as His daughter could I have submitted and become persistently determined to face even giants like the topic of suicide by means of introducing these concepts of *Stewardship of Wellbeing* and *Stewardship of Mind.*

Nothing New

When we pursue answers, we find in our searching that there is nothing new under the sun. An approach or recent documentation might *seem* to be new, but God knows differently. Perhaps even though little has been heard to date on the topics of stewardship as it pertains to overall wellness and the mind, believers will now be ignited to act upon the awareness of the need through the lens of scripture. May more be done to research and pursue how the exercise of good hermeneutics, solid theology, and empirical data further supports what experiential testimonies declare. How fearfully and wonderfully created we are has yet to be boldly proclaimed in the context of speaking out concerning the stigmatized, awkward topics that leave so many squirming in the church. We must live unashamed that something in life was or is so painful that sometimes even a Christian can do ungodly things. Those who are in this pain have no, or very little support from God's family in the healing process. This must stop.

In 2007, Dean Ornish, M.D. published a book called *The Spectrum: A Scientifically Proven Program to Feel Better, Live Longer, Lose Weight, Gain Health.* This is the earliest mention found on the concept of the *Stewardship of Wellness* as a coined phrase. This, along with other books, addresses how our health is improved and better maintained through diet, exercise, and overall input. Many have since expounded on the topic of wellness from other perspectives. In his book, Ornish states that "how you eat, how much you exercise, how you manage stress, and how you live" contribute to being well. "Because it's based on pleasure, not pain; abundance, not deprivation; science, not myth; freedom and power, not restriction and manipulation. The joy of living is sustainable; fear of dying is not. This is about how to enjoy life more fully while enhancing your health and well-being. You can actually change how your genes are expressed just by changing what you eat and how you live."

Pleasure has nothing to do with the fleshly, hedonistic desires found within a prosperity gospel. God's desire from the start was and is that we enjoy a life free of suffering in full communion with Him, the Almighty God. In time, that state of existence will return. For now, we are stewards of what He created. When we partner with the Creator, we co-create. That is to say, we align what we create according to God's blueprint and not without His vision and intended growth.

God did not give Noah the ark as a means of survival and victory. God gave Noah verbal instructions so that Noah realized the blueprint as a means of God's provision for salvation. The details for the ark were the result of Noah's fellowship and communication with God, but notice that Noah did not possess further specifics or a map for navigation once the ark was afloat in unchartered waters. Noah and his family got in, and then God controlled the ark. We are vessels handcrafted by God, and Jesus is our ark. The Holy Spirit is our navigation and it is meant to be that God Almighty is at the helm of our ship; our "relation-ship."

To achieve this is to seize the opportunity to become all that He has proposed for us to be.

We won't live here forever, but we can live well and increasingly thrive as we progress in our lives on earth. Improvement is always possible. Rebuilding the temple at Jerusalem is not a mere historical narrative.

> *From that day on, half of my servants carried on the work while half of them held the spears, the shields, the bows and the breastplates; and the captains were behind the whole house of Judah. 17 Those who were rebuilding the wall and those who carried burdens took their load with one hand doing the work and the other holding a weapon. 18 As for the builders, each wore his sword girded at his side as he built, while the trumpeter stood near me."*
> — Nehemiah 4:16-18

This story has personal application when we replace the Jerusalem temple with our own bodies as the temple. Our bodies are God's temples. As it was then, rebuilding today might result in a battle. It is a project well worth equipping ourselves for and taking up weapons[16] as necessary to ensure we are fully arrayed in the armor of God. As scripture teaches, not only do we have God's protection, as the temple of the Holy Spirit we are stewards of maintaining the dwelling of the Most High God.

> *...so that you will be able to stand firm against the schemes of the devil. [12] For our struggle is not against flesh and blood, but against the rulers, against the powers, against the world forces of this darkness, against the spiritual forces of wickedness in the heavenly places. [13] Therefore, take up the full armor of God, so that you will be able to resist in the evil day, and having done everything, to stand firm. [14] Stand firm therefore, having girded your loins with truth, and having put on the breastplate of righteousness, [15] and having shod your feet with the preparation of the gospel of peace; [16] in addition to all, taking up the shield of faith with which you will be able to extinguish all the flaming arrows of the evil one. [17] And take the helmet of salvation, and the sword of the Spirit, which is the word of God.*
>
> — Ephesians 6:11-17

The benefit of living well is joy, peace, and the blessing of standing on God's promises with the assurance that all is well with one's soul.

Others, like renowned communication pathologist and cognitive neuroscientist, Dr. Caroline Leaf, who has specialized in cognitive and metacognitive neuropsychology since the early 1980s, have researched the mind-brain connection, the nature of mental health, and the formation of memory. She was one of the first in her field to study how the brain can change (neuroplasticity) with directed mind input. This affirms and aligns with what scripture says concerning our ability to be transformed by the renewal of our mind. Transformation is available. To achieve it personally

---

16 2 Corinthians 10:3-5 *For though we walk in the flesh, we do not war according to the flesh, [4] for the weapons of our warfare are not of the flesh, but divinely powerful for the destruction of fortresses. [5] We are destroying speculations and every lofty thing raised up against the knowledge of God, and we are taking every thought captive to the obedience of Christ.*

comes as a direct result of applied alignment with our Creator who created us in His perfect image. Submission to God, while harder for some than others, is not the hardest part of transforming your life. Aligning with Him, the one who created you, means you trust that He is able to renew and transform you. This trust can be more difficult for some. The simplicity is that we abide in the truth.

As a passionate Christian and scientist, Dr. Leaf provides practical and applicable information about what happens in the brain when we seek God first and transform. It comes by where we fix our thoughts, how we consider our feelings, and what choices we make.

Think about your dietary intake and the importance of maintaining proper nutrition. This principle applies to what we feed our minds. Citing Daniel and the author of Hebrews, Dr. Leaf says, "In the context of our unique situations, and like, Daniel, in the Babylonian court, find a way of eating that is God-centered, enabling us to carry output God's will (Daniel 1). We are fearfully and wonderfully made, and our uniqueness pervades every part of our lives including what we eat. We, like Daniel and his companions, have to find a way of eating that suits us so that we can run the race set before us (Hebrews 12:1)."

Scripture likens how the maturation of a believer is like an infant craving pure milk.[17] Time and spiritual progression as you walk with God and apply His word in your life should result in more substantive consumption,[18] giving you the ability to carry out His commission, which starts with making disciples. As a believer becomes more like Christ, you learn to appreciate Him in complete awe of how wonderfully designed your body is and how wonder-

---

17 1 Peter 2:2-3 *Like newborn babies, crave pure spiritual milk, so that by it you may grow up in your salvation, 3 now that you have tasted that the Lord is good.*

18 Hebrew 5:12-14 *"In fact, though by this time you ought to be teachers, you need someone to teach you the elementary truths of God's word all over again. You need milk, not solid food! 13 Anyone who lives on milk, being still an infant, is not acquainted with the teaching about righteousness. 14 But solid food is for the mature, who by constant use have trained themselves to distinguish good from evil."*

fully designed the entire body of the church is. The outcome is that it is possible to love God completely and serve others selflessly.[19]

WARFARE

It is important to know the "what, when, where, how, and why" of the warfare that is part of life. The stakes are high—it is you! You are the treasure desired by God. You are desired by God because He created you and He loves you. We are all born captive by the ramification of Adam and Eve's deception.[20] One of God's creations, Lucifer (Satan, the devil, our enemy), rose up in pride and arrogance, coveting the power of God[21] to become a deceitful counterfeit.[22]

The battle can be subtle, confusing, or fierce. Beloved, be encouraged that while there may be battles, the war is already won.

> *When the perishable has been clothed with the imperishable, and the mortal with immortality, then the saying that is written will come true: "Death has been swallowed up in victory."* [55] *"Where, O death, is your victory? Where, O death, is your sting?"* [56] *The sting of death is sin, and the power of sin is the law.*
>
> — 1 Corinthians 15:54-56

---

19 Deuteronomy 6:5 *"Love the Lord your God with all your heart and with all your soul and with all your strength."*

20 Romans 3:23 *"for all have sinned and fall short of the glory of God,"*

21 Isaiah 14:11-13 *"How you have fallen from heaven, morning star, son of the dawn! You have been cast down to the earth, you who once laid low the nations* [13] *You said in your heart, "I will ascend to the heavens; I will raise my throne above the stars of God; I will sit enthroned on the mount of assembly, on the utmost heights of Mount Zaphon."*

22 2 Corinthians 11:13-15 *"For such people are false apostles, deceitful workers, masquerading as apostles of Christ.* [14] *And no wonder, for Satan himself masquerades as an angel of light.* [15] *It is not surprising, then, if his servants also masquerade as servants of righteousness. Their end will be what their actions deserve."*

Victory is in Christ and was completed at the cross[23] with the precious blood of God's perfect lamb. He Himself declared it.

METHOD OF OPERATION

The enemy is crafty[24] but quite simple in his method of operation! Satan is the father of lies.[25] He perpetually and relentlessly accuses.[26] He does not cease and is constantly on the prowl seeking whom to devour.[27] The method is simple: lies and accusations. This betrayal is treachery. The way spiritual warfare is carried out is strategic. He does not act alone but is the prince of the power of the air. Basically, he has nothing he can grasp, unless one embraces and allows for his toxic infestation of the mind, body, and soul. When and how he implements his methods of operation are carried out with a strategy.

STRATEGY

Strategy always includes a process. Its direction is focused on the end goal and desired results. As it is with any other organization, a successful strategy requires many parties to act in one accord to accomplish the vision set forth by its leadership. Satan did not act alone to pursue ultimate reign over God's creation. He had followers, and those followers are the spiritual and demonic force that come against the human soul. That said, we need not fear a demon around every corner or under every bush. He does

---

23 John 19:30 *"When he had received the drink, Jesus said, "It is finished." With that, he bowed his head and gave up his spirit."*

24 Genesis 3:1 *"Now the serpent was more crafty than any of the wild animals the Lord God had made."*

25 John 8:44 *"You belong to your father, the devil, and you want to carry out your father's desires. He was a murderer from the beginning, not holding to the truth, for there is no truth in him. When he lies, he speaks his native language, for he is a liar and the father of lies."*

26 Revelation 12:10 *"... the accuser of our brothers and sisters..."*

27 1 Peter 5:8 *"Be alert and of sober mind. Your enemy the devil prowls around like a roaring lion looking for someone to devour."*

not geographically have the occupation of that much territory. Keep in mind a territory is tangible, the air is not. Air encompasses all the earth; hence spiritual warfare exists but is also geographic. This precept is found in the vision of a man from Daniel 10. The mention of what detained answer to Daniel's prayer indicates spiritual warfare in a clearly geographic depiction of spiritual battles by geographic assignment and forfeiture when God's people give up what is theirs to keep.

Temptation is part of the strategy of deception. By temptation, the enemy lures a weary, heavy-laden, or vulnerable suspect and preys upon him until the mission of killing, stealing, and destroying comes to fruition. We see it in the life of Christ when He was led into the wilderness to be tempted.[28] The temptations faced by Christ and overcome by Him were necessary so that His people, too, may overcome temptation that is common to man. God does provide a way out from temptation.[29] Our enemy is relentless, however, and a weary soul becomes vulnerable to fall prey to the devil's schemes. Forgiveness is not only a gift received, but it is one we must continually practice, lest we provide a place of vulnerability for the enemy, who is all too ready to wreak havoc by means of subtly making temptation palatable.[30]

As it is written in Proverbs 14:12 and 6:25: *"There is a way which seems right to a man, but its end is the way of death."* Therefore, the precepts of being alert, rested, well, fit, and in good health are important to the stewardship of wellbeing.

---

28 Matthew 4:1 and Luke 4:1 *"Then Jesus was led by the Spirit into the wilderness to be tempted by the devil."*

29 1 Corinthians 10:13 *"No temptation has overtaken you except what is common to mankind. And God is faithful; he will not let you be tempted beyond what you can bear. But when you are tempted, he will also provide a way out so that you can endure it."*

30 2 Corinthians 2:10-11 *"10 But one whom you forgive anything, I forgive also; for indeed what I have forgiven, if I have forgiven anything, I did it for your sakes in the presence of Christ, 11 so that no advantage would be taken of us by Satan, for we are not ignorant of his schemes."*

GOAL

Our mortal enemy seeks to kill, steal, and destroy. He does so in many different ways like stealing joy or dashing hopes with unmet expectations or things hoped for. The very situation of experiencing hope deferred leads to a sick heart. When the heart is sick, so goes our thinking, and amplified emotions can lead us astray. We do not remain fixed on Jesus.

> *Therefore, since we have so great a cloud of witnesses surrounding us, let us also lay aside every encumbrance and the sin which so easily entangles us, and let us run with endurance the race that is set before us, ² fixing our eyes on Jesus, the author and perfecter of faith, who for the joy set before Him endured the cross, despising the shame, and has sat down at the right hand of the throne of God. ³ For consider Him who has endured such hostility by sinners against Himself, so that you will not grow weary and lose heart.*
>
> — Hebrews 12:1-3

Hope deferred can compromise one's well being. The enemy's goal is to take out God's people any way that he can. With him, there is no sanctity of life. It is all-out war! He is clever and knowledgeable of God's word:

> *¹⁸ But someone may well say, "You have faith and I have works; show me your faith without the works, and I will show you my faith by my works." ¹⁹ You believe that God is one. You do well; the demons also believe, and shudder. ²⁰ But are you willing to recognize, you foolish fellow, that faith without works is useless?*
>
> James 2:18-20

The devil will use God's word with subtle deviation from the whole truth in order to sway right thinking, misguide one's emotions, and to keep unhealed wounds open. The fact that Christ is for us means that we be one with God.

> *I ask on their behalf; I do not ask on behalf of the world, but of those whom You have given Me; for they are Yours; ¹⁰ and all*

things that are Mine are Yours, and Yours are Mine; and I have been glorified in them. ¹¹ I am no longer in the world; and yet they themselves are in the world, and I come to You. Holy Father, keep them in Your name, the name which You have given Me, that they may be one even as We are. ¹² While I was with them, I was keeping them in Your name which You have given Me; and I guarded them and not one of them perished but the son of perdition, so that the Scripture would be fulfilled.

— John 17:9-12.

The enemy works through things God hates: divorce, insobriety, anger, rage, malice, sexual immorality, suicide, homicide, genocide, conflicted gender, and fleshly lust of being something other than what one was created perfectly to be. You are worth the fight. Were it not so, Jesus would not have done for us what we could not do for ourselves.

He made Him who knew no sin to be sin on our behalf, so that we might become the righteousness of God in Him.

— 2 Corinthians 5:21

Concerning the enemy,

and they were not strong enough, and there was no longer a place found for them in heaven. And the great dragon was thrown down, the serpent of old who is called the devil and Satan, who deceives the whole world; he was thrown down to the earth, and his angels were thrown down with him. Then I heard a loud voice in heaven, saying, "Now the salvation, and the power, and the kingdom of our God and the authority of His Christ have come, for the accuser of our brethren has been thrown down, he who accuses them before our God day and night.

— Revelation 12:8-10

God provides redemption[31] for all humanity who will confess Him and believe that Jesus Christ is Lord. In Christ alone we have

---

31 1 Corinthians 6:20 *"For you have been bought with a price: therefore glorify God in your body."*

the eternal assurance of reconciliation to a pure and holy fellowship, as it was in the beginning, is and will continue, until full restoration of all that God created in the beginning is complete.

> *"He who overcomes, I will make him a pillar in the temple of My God, and he will not go out from it anymore; and I will write on him the name of My God, and the name of the city of My God, the new Jerusalem, which comes down out of heaven from My God, and My new name."*
>
> — Revelation 3:12

Victory is in Christ and for us by the blood of the lamb. By testimony,[32] we take the first steps in discipling someone else, through study of God's work, we learn how to test what is of God and what is not. We grow and we gain wisdom concerning what it means to make disciples.

MARCHING ORDERS

The marching orders for God's people are clear: make disciples, baptize, teach, and rest assured that we are not alone in what has been entrusted to the church to accomplish. Namely that:

> *"This gospel of the kingdom shall be preached in the whole world as a testimony to all the nations, and then the end will come."*
>
> — Matthew 24:14

The church is responsible to disciple no matter what the subject, despite any awkwardness, and with all authority. Even Judas Iscariot was called by Jesus to follow Him. How he betrayed Christ is not a point upon which to build a theology about suicide, when there are many ambiguities to his final actions which led to his desperate act. The words of Christ are that none was lost except the one destined to fulfill Scripture.

---

32 Revelation 12:11 *"And they overcame him because of the blood of the Lamb and because of the word of their testimony, and they did not love their life even when faced with death."*

Food for thought,

> *But even the archangel Michael, when he was disputing with*
> *the devil about the body of Moses, did not himself dare to condemn*
> *him for slander but said, "The Lord rebuke you!"*
>
> — Jude 9

May the Lord not rebuke a single soul for remaining silent about any subject or crisis that results in the assault of His people. The church and its individual members are responsible for how and what we disciple. We are to speak the truth in love and give a reason for what we believe. We can trust that the truth of God's word will not return void, but rather, it will accomplish the purpose for which it is sent.

The church must step up and disciple on some tough subjects, including the importance of the *Stewardship of Wellness* and *Stewardship of Mind*. As the end draws near, the battle and impact on minds not well-maintained are evident in the ever-increasing statistics of preventable deaths.

The church much face the fact that the surviving family members of a death by suicide or one who has attempted suicide and his or her family members are experiencing extreme spiritual warfare. Can we leave them unattended? No! The enemy loves to deal a final blow on wounded souls. He steals their future and destroys so much in the lives of those who survive such a misguided loss. The church must do better. Go forth and face this giant with every confidence. God is on your side!

Having presented stewardship in a broader sense prepares you for the next brick in the foundation set forth to better love one another. Through self-evaluation of attitudes and examination of scripture, the prayerful outcome is that we become better stewards in suicide prevention. Wellness, especially of the mind our Lord has given each of us, are worthy of care and stewardship. The topic of suicide is one of pain and confusion. As such, scripture gives so much hope. Knowing that Messiah is familiar with pain, if we will, we can trust him to heal our wounds (Isaiah 53:3). Scripture is full of powerful reminders that God is greater than all sin. Four main questions from Isaiah 50:2

> *"When I came, why was there no one? When I called, why was there no one to answer? Was my arm too short to deliver you? Do I lack the strength to rescue you?"*

begs answers and a few chapters later, God gives answers with hope.

> *Behold, the Lord's hand is not so short that it cannot save; Nor is His ear so dull that it cannot hear. ² But your wrongdoings have caused a separation between you and your God, and your sins have hidden His face from you so that He does not hear.*
> — Isaiah 59: 1-2

God's heart on the matter of sin or wrongdoing is that none perish, but that all would turn to Him and be saved.[33] God is able and always invites people to turn to him. There is hope.[34] The next and last brick in laying the foundation will take us from stewardship into the mystery of the unknown. The next flaming arrow of truth pierces to the core of what occurs that leads to suicide and it is founds as a biblical definition right out of scripture. With all we question following such a tragedy, these are certainties. Suicide is trust in confusion, spoken lies (listened to), and conceived mischief that brings forth iniquity. This definition comes straight from our Heavenly Father.[35] It is that father of lies that confuses. God brings order. Our enemy fosters mischief and leads people into iniquity.

---

33 *"The Lord is not slow about His promise, as some count slowness, but is patient toward you, not wishing for any to perish but for all to come to repentance."* — 2 Peter 3:9

34 *"My sheep listen to my voice; I know them, and they follow me. ²⁸ I give them eternal life, and they shall never perish; no one will snatch them out of my hand. ²⁹ My Father, who has given them to me, is greater than all; no one can snatch them out of my Father's hand. ³⁰ I and the Father are one."* — John 10:27-30

35 *"No one sues righteously and no one pleads honestly. They trust in confusion and speak lies; They conceive mischief and bring forth iniquity."* — Isaiah 59:4

God provides a way through any crisis.[36] Were it not for revelation, we may miss so much the Lord has to offer.

---

36 *"No temptation has overtaken you except what is common to mankind. And God is faithful; he will not let you be tempted beyond what you can bear. But when you are tempted, he will also provide a way out so that you can endure it."* — 1 Corinthians 10:13.

MYSTERY OF THE UNKNOWN

When questions remain unanswered, the brokenhearted and crushed soul struggles with an innate and vehement longing to know what it cannot understand. When circumstances are beyond comprehension, the perceived need for answers is amplified. A lack of answers poses challenges that prolong mending broken hearts, complicating one's grief. Processing grief and recovery leads to great angst, especially in situations that involve preventable behavior that compromises health and threatens life. Any form of suicidal behavior, be it self-harm or sudden death seeming to be out of nowhere, leads to deep wounds in survivors. The behavior of one person impacts others. Tragically, and perhaps erroneously, when death by suicide happens, the common conclusion is that the act was nothing less than selfish. Consider that there could be another perspective. Who in the church asks survivors of suicide attempts how they can be ministered to more effectively? It is time to seek to know what we do not know; it could be quite the breakthrough in crisis ministry.

The inability to have answers is seldom satisfactory for a survivor. Even partial answers do not suffice. Partial answers, like notes that were left behind, leave the bereaved weighed down by a need for information that is logical and reasonable. Because it is hard for anyone to know what the deceased person was thinking, it is not possible to gain complete answers. Are we really ready and willing to ask questions and to learn to discern with spiritual eyes and ears? We must, if we desire the Holy Spirit to guide us into all truth to bring light into the darkness of suicide. Here is a striking consideration: Suicide can be the culmination of many circumstances the church already minsters to, including, but not limited to, economic crisis, health crisis, and divorce. If this is the case, the church is missing incredible opportunities to prevent what no one desires to happen on their watch. So why does the church disappear once despair has escalated to loss of life?

CONSPICUOUS

Stigma and shame are thieves. Both threaten, assault, and rob the security of one's God-given identity. Both devalue life, when clearly God loves and is near the brokenhearted and crushed in spirit. God does not kick the wounded; He meets people where they are. Sad and differently, hurt people hurt other people, creating a vicious cycle that is hard to break. It takes courage and strength to humble oneself before the Father with one's confession of self-inflicted wounds for the purpose of healing. We must be willing to be vulnerable and face head-on the accusations of the enemy that murmur in the thoughts of the person that got to such a low point. People would rather speculate about what happened and gossip than open up a willingness to ask an attempt survivor: "What could you share with me that might help me help you or someone else in the future?" The church should be shaken up by the fact that Jesus chose to die in the place of the one who has attempted suicide to redeem even the shortcoming of ending one's life. This should move the church out of ambiguity and reluctance of specific or targeted ministry that impacts so many in the community. Even in his tragic end, Judas actually had a role in the fulfillment of scripture, according to Jesus himself.

> *"While I was with them, I was keeping them in Your name which You have given Me; and I guarded them and not one of them perished but the son of perdition, so that the Scripture would be fulfilled."*
>
> — John 17:12

Shame and stigma create toxic thoughts and conditions. They promote behavior contrary to edifying and lifting others out of miry pits. Stigma and shame perpetuate the cycle of labeling, profiling, or insisting that once the brokenness of any suicidal thought or act is out in the open, life will forever be broken. They project onto a wounded soul that they are not fit to become anything other than the stigma. They assault one's identity and shroud hope that God can redeem such a person. These lies are just not true!

INCONSPICUOUS

I wrote this book as one convicted and compelled, much like a watchman's job description as found in Ezekiel. Enough is enough! Every life matters. Those perishing as a result of a death that might have been prevented must stop, or we will each give account for what was not done.

> *And the word of the Lord came to me, saying, ² "Son of man, speak to the sons of your people and say to them, 'If I bring a sword upon a land, and the people of the land take one man from among them and make him their watchman, ³ and he sees the sword coming upon the land and blows on the trumpet and warns the people, ⁴ then he who hears the sound of the trumpet and does not take warning, and a sword comes and takes him away, his blood will be on his own head. ⁵ He heard the sound of the trumpet but did not take warning; his blood will be on himself. But had he taken warning, he would have delivered his life. ⁶ But if the watchman sees the sword coming and does not blow the trumpet and the people are not warned, and a sword comes and takes a person from them, he is taken away in his iniquity; but his blood I will require from the watchman's hand.'*
> — Ezekiel 33:1-6

A watchman gives a warning, alerting people to something in need of attention or else it will impact the entire community. He prays for the call at hand and knows his mission is to provide every notification that there is an opportunity to prepare and take action accordingly. Once aware, individuals and the community can take action to prevent what the church finds so hard to minister through or discuss: suicide. Brothers and sisters of the church, if we do not humble ourselves and face this giant, we are no better than what scripture has to say about one who does not provide:

> *But if anyone does not provide for his own, and especially for those of his household, he has denied the faith and is worse than an unbeliever.*
>
> — 1 Timothy 5:8

The numbers of how many people are impacted by suicide are staggering. According to the World Health Organization, suicide is the second leading cause of death among teens and young adults. If younger generations are the future, and the church does nothing to come alongside them for the battle for their lives, the church is no better than a herd who runs away from a hungry lion leaving their most vulnerable open to attack. While this is a metaphor, it has also been explained this way by a number of suicide survivors who are now doing their best not only to survive, but to heal. They feel like the herd of God-fearing Christians willing to see them through this valley of the shadow of death has scattered. While many speak of the number of fatalities, few are aware of the ratio of thirty to one. This is the number of attempts, which by grace and thanks be to God, are not successful.

Commit

If only we knew how words and circumstances affect those carrying invisible wounds. Wounds created when the police show up and a scene is secured to rule out foul play. Wounds made when the yellow tape comes out and everyone, other than responders working the scene, is removed from the area. Wounds deepened as the family grasps into the nothingness of a full-on tsunami of emotions that come with the grief associated with sudden loss. For the devastated family and friends impacted, it is incomprehensible. Also, there is often denial of death because suicide is not something we ever think is possible for someone we loved.

It is well-known that when crime happens, someone "committed" the crime. The phrase "committed suicide" carries complexity very difficult to grasp where it involves the perspective of surviving family members and those who survive an attempt. It feels like a crime; the scene is taped off and investigation ensues. There are cameras, detectives, a medical examiner who will eventually arrive, and of course, there are police, paramedics, and fire personnel assigned to the scene; maybe a chaplain or advocate has been dispatched to help with the family. When the word "committed" is heard, denial escalates emotions. Why? Because the word "committed" is associated with a crime. Crimes are bad, and "bad" can be taken to mean that that their loved one *is bad* or *did something bad*. As denial escalates, many thoughts escalate among them, including any spiritual considerations of what the suicide (or suicide attempt) means according to one's belief system.

As a new perspective, consider the use of the word "commit" in this context as poor stewardship for the Christian. The general public is careless and unknowingly harmful with verbiage where spiritual warfare factors into the situation. The enemy will use the word "committed" with full verbal assault of lies and accusations, and the weary soul finds no reprieve. Reprieve can come, however, if the truth is spoken into the chaotic darkness of self-talk. We can keep others from slipping into the abyss and embracing the lies.

Shifting your perspective does not mean suicide is condoned. The perspective sheds light as a voice of advocacy for those struggling to heal beyond the tragedy that stigmatizes and can negatively follow one's reputation. It is often other people who will not let a hurting person move into the future of hope with the promise of restoration. Do not let that person be you!

While there are some places where suicide is a legitimate crime, the penalty in those areas is not known nor was it deemed relevant to this book. One could argue that the moral injury from which one must recover self inflicted and following the act of attempting suicide it can feel like a form of life sentence; yet, it is not beyond God's grace, and forgivness. For man it is more difficult. When someone acts to take his life and survives it, there is a very long and lonely road ahead of him; a road on which the enemy of our souls is salivating, snarling, and growling all manners of noise. The noise is very difficult to silence, unless one learns to fix his eyes on God. They may even feel hurt that God saved them from the despair of dying that day, that way, and that hurt needs help to heal.

SURVIVAL

Survival does not start until the moment that one's mental faculty realizes what did *not* happen; the moment of regaining consciousness. The person realizes in a moment of groggy shock that he or she is still alive. It is then that the emotional, behavioral, and spiritual reality confronts the person. The mode of survival a body is in during the early regaining of consciousness means psychologically the reason "why" is likely not completely clear to the person as to why they did what they did. Uncharacteristic reactions can occur that may or may not be remembered by the survivor. Such behavior will not be forgotten by those present. Giving someone full compassion when they are stable is critical to their future healing.

A person who survives an attempt may feel like he has just been sentenced to prison. It is like being in a prison cell with a wanted felon; a murderous cellmate who will not shut up! The devil is his cellmate; the prison is his mind. His cellmate wants him dead. He may wish he were. His community is stunned that someone they know tried to kill himself. His nearest relationships may be present, but all the while wondering, "Will he live, or is he going to die?" That feeling changes as the hurt sinks into each broken heart unable to understand the many questions running through their minds.

Here is what can be done. Remain present. The hurt and awkwardness of being uncomfortable about how you feel is no doubt significant. It is not a lessened feeling, but know that it is quite likely far different than can be imagined, unless you too have lived experience. The person who has attempted to take his life needs to know he is not alone in the fight *for* his life. Your presence is powerful, just show up and be consistent. The uncomfortableness felt is a huge opportunity for growth, as growth never happens in a comfort zone. Resist the temptation to flee. Resist the devil and he, with his temptation, will flee. Clothe yourself in Christ. Be a servant. Sometimes the most powerful gift is to be available when someone's sense of vulnerability heightens the fear surrounding the situation. God did not give you a spirit of fear. Again, this is spiritual warfare as much as it is mental health in need of recovery.

If believers would commit to change our language and realize the power of our words, it would make a difference. When words of life are spoken and backed up by proof in scripture, you have a powerful weapon to give to a soul in need of encouragement. You have truth that can pierce the chaotic darkness.

SUPPORT

Surviving a suicide attempt is a fight! A person must find desire after waking up, with every consequence of knowing that God said, "No, not today." If something led to the pain and desperation so as to act to end life, know that the pain of realizing the pit one finds himself in after an attempt is ineffable. I cannot imagine anyone ever wanting to be in such a conundrum. The onslaught of enemy warfare rages with every manner of trash talk, and some of it comes from the community also wounded by the attempts. Support is needed and it is not as available to the proportion of pain it causes. It seems hurt lashes out of its pain rather than to reach out of our pain into someone's hemorrhaging soul. Just like a person bleeding out, the shock of injury often renders the injured incapable of placing on his or her own tourniquet. When a wound is invisible, internal, and has injured the soul, there is no one better to come alongside in compassion and non-judgmental care than a servant of Christ. He heals the hurt of all those injured by a single attempt to end life. It takes coming together and realizing that when God said, "No" to the end of life, He said, "Yes" to another chance to do things His way and discover more about Him than could ever have been, had the hurt not been surrendered.

Are you guilty of saying things like: "What a selfish person," "What a failure or loser," "He couldn't even get that right"? What is preventable in this situation is breaking the stronghold of the lies that paralyze and cause hesitancy to champion the need to do better in ministry. Scripture teaches that the tongue has the power of life and death. Such things may not be said straight to one's face, but they are spoken, sometimes in earshot, behind one's back, or coming back around as a rumor conveyed by a concerned "friend." Why does it stop there? The Christian must speak life into the wounded person. Show them where in scripture God speaks of our value[37] and how God sees our brokenness.[38] Brokenness is redeemable, and it takes the redeemed to reinforce what the enemy is ferociously attacking. The only evidence of damage comes when the casualty occurs. Silence causes just as much damage as opinions coming from the secondarily injured that heap caustic words by means of godless chatter[39] from one hurt person to another hurt person. It is like heaping salt into a gaping injury.

It is wrong thinking that discussion will increase the risk of someone taking negative action. It is in error to think that open conversations and question-answer conversations that include compassion and authentic interest to learn what might help each individual won't help. We must not believe that conversation should

---

37   John 15:13 *"Greater love has no one than this, that one lay down his life for his friends."*

1 Corinthians 6:20 *"For you have been bought with a price: therefore glorify God in your body."*

1 Timothy 2:6 *"who gave Himself as a ransom for all, the testimony given at the proper time."*

38   Isaiah 42:3 *"A bruised reed He will not break And a dimly burning wick He will not extinguish; He will faithfully bring forth justice."*

39   2 Timothy 2:15-17a *"Be diligent to present yourself approved to God as a workman who does not need to be ashamed, accurately handling the word of truth. 16 But avoid worldly and empty chatter, for it will lead to further ungodliness, 17 and their talk will spread like gangrene."*

be hushed or that reporting on the tragedy of a first responder that lost his life in the line of duty because the death was by suicide is glamorizing it. That family suffers many losses surrounding such a death, among them the honor due to a servant's family for all their loved one did to serve which ultimately cost his life.

Some answers exist within those with lived experience. When we muster the guts to be strong and courageous, we may prevent another life from ending. It is natural to want to know, so what keeps people gripped in silent angst and not asking questions of those with the best chance of providing insight?

Understanding

Scripture tells us not to lean on our own understanding. Still, we often try to wrap our minds around something so painful it is even hard for survivors to verbalize. Answers do not typically satisfy or help a wounded soul reconcile a moral injury. What should we know that those with lived experience wish that others either knew or would ask?

Differences

Not every attempt at or death by suicide is the result of chronic mental illness. Examples of this include acts of desperation during the Great Depression when the stock market crashed, scores of lives ended by individual volition, as it was with the atrocity of the Jonestown mass suicide when cult followers took the Kool-Aid and drank, and the fall out of the 2015, Ashley Madison list that exposed individuals involved in extramarital affairs that resulted in the death of a seminary professor.[40] Acts of desperation are a contributing factor in suicide. A person in so much pain and turmoil can be helped and so often there are volunteers and ministers caring

---

40 https://baptistnews.com/article/family-says-professor-s-death-a-suicide/#. X4sOJy9h2uU "Since then, authorities in Toronto have said they're investigating suicides that could be linked to the data dump."

for people through hard circumstances without much consideration given to the cumulative toll it can take.

The previous examples demonstrate how wrong assumptions can lead to profile and conclude that every suicide is a result of mental illness. Can it be the result of a temporary break in mental health? Yes! Scripture incites believers to maintain a sober mind. Without sobriety or clarity of mind, be it emotional or psychological, there is a compromise with risks. The risks of consequences that come when you do not take the time to value the importance of stewarding mental health. More presentation programs need to be taught in the church from a biblical perspective and must include the voice of those healed and with lived experience. Those with lived experience should not be limited to family and friends of those who attempted or died at their own hands. Insight is most complete when those with testimonies of recovery can participate. It is part of healing, and it provides participants an opportunity in a designated setting to engage in asking questions.

It is imperative to ask the questions of those that are living in victory, and if you are one who is, break out of the darkness and let God's marvelous light shine through you.

PERDITION

Scripture gives glimpses to what it would be like for the betrayer of Christ. The church and its theologians have concluded many things about Judas but finding something that addressed the topic of possible repentance and or redemption concerning Judas. Moreover and relevant to the contemporary problem of sucide, Scripture is silent about life beyond an attempt. However, God's sovereignty, attributes, and truths are consistent and true.Scripture made the comparison of such a tormenting situation for the one to betray Christ, that it would be better to have a millstone around his neck and thrown into the sea. Such torment is unfathomable unless one has been there. Left unattended chronic trauma stress and desperation contribute to compromised mental health and suicide risk.[41]

ANOMALIES

It bears mention and much consideration of what scriptures say concerning Judas Iscariot. He is called the "son of perdition" and dependent on what version or translation one uses, it may indicate the "one destined to perish." He was chosen by God and called by Jesus to be a disciple.

Let's look with detail at John 17:

---

41 "The risk of trauma exposure, and the subsequent psychological reaction to that exposure, has played a role in the human experience throughout our history as a species. Within the past several decades, the clinical and therapeutic orientation toward diagnosis and treatment for posttraumatic stress disorder (PTSD) has shifted progressively from a sole focus on physical threat and fear-based anxiety to a more inclusive acknowledgement of psychological symptoms that affect trauma survivors (Friedman et al. 2011). Moral injury, which accompanies about one third of combat-related PTSD cases (Bryan et al. 2018; Frankfurt and Frazier 2016; Stein et al. 2012), involves the emotional, behavioral, and spiritual sequelae of exposure to events that challenge cherished values and beliefs (Litz et al. 2009). Symptoms of moral injury include guilt, shame, loss of meaning/purpose, loss of trust in self, others or Deity, depression, anxiety, anger, re-experiencing moral conflict, suicidal ideation/behavior, self-injury, social withdrawal, re-orienting of value systems, and impaired interpersonal functioning (Jinkerson 2016; Litz et al. 2009; Maguen et al. 2009; Steenkamp and Litz 2013; Wisco et al. 2017; Zimmermann et al. 2016). Furthermore, co-occurrence of PTSD and moral injury is associated with increased risk for suicide (Bryan et al. 2018)." Such evidence must not be ignored by ministry leaders. Moral injury is at the core of silence in the church and outcry of those impacted of how important the church is in suicide prevention. God's people have not been given a spirit of fear. What is fear based may have spiritual origins and could be consequential or contributory to imbalances of mind, body, and or soul. Without a more holistic, meaning, to include spiritual conversations and restoration where mental illness is concerned the whole man is limited in his ability to recover from and reconcile trauma and its impact on his life. God never wastes a hurt. He uses restored, once broken people to impact others.

"13 But now I come to You; and these things I speak in the world so that they may have My joy made full in themselves. 14 I have given them Your word; and the world has hated them, because they are not of the world, even as I am not of the world. 15 I do not ask You to take them out of the world, but to keep them from the evil one. 16 They are not of the world, even as I am not of the world. 17 Sanctify them in the truth; Your word is truth. 18 As You sent Me into the world, I also have sent them into the world. 19 For their sakes I sanctify Myself, that they themselves also may be sanctified in truth. 20 "I do not ask on behalf of these alone, but for those also who believe in Me through their word; 21 that they may all be one; even as You, Father, are in Me and I in You, that they also may be in Us, so that the world may believe that You sent Me."

— John 17:13-21

Note who is talking. Jesus is praying to the Father for the twelve.

He does it so they may have joy made complete. Does that include Judas? According to verse 6 earlier in the passage maybe there is something we don't understand concerning Judas' demise.

"I have manifested Your name to the men whom You gave Me out of the world; they were Yours and You gave them to Me, and they have kept Your word."

If they were God's and no one can snatch someone from the hand of Christ,

"My sheep hear My voice, and I know them, and they follow Me; 28 and I give eternal life to them, and they will never perish; and no one will snatch them out of My hand. 29 My Father, who has given them to Me, is greater than all; and no one is able to snatch them out of the Father's hand."

— John 10:27-29

Five anomalies that are contrary to beliefs held about Judas:

–   Jesus prays for *"My joy made full in themselves."* (v13)

- Jesus has given God's word (v14)
- Jesus prays that *"they be kept from the evil one."* (v15)
- Jesus prays that they be sanctified in the truth he has given (v17)
- Jesus sanctifies Himself so that they too may be sanctified in truth.

The phrase son of perdition is attributed as a Hebrew idiom for one destined to perish.

The New International Version translates the phrase as 'the one doomed to destruction.' D. A. Carson suggests that this verse refers both to Judas' character and to his destiny. However, it must not be overlooked that a similar phrase in the Hebrew text, such as 'sons of corruption' in Isaiah 1:4 בָּנִים מַשְׁחִיתִים *banim mashchitim* create quite a gap of where the church has fallen into ambiguity. The exact Hebrew or Greek term 'son of perdition' does not occur in Jewish writings before the New Testament.

The two occurrences of the Greek phrase have traditionally been translated consistently in English Bibles, following the Latin Vulgate which has *'filius perditionis'* (son of perdition) in both instances. However, this is not the case in all languages; for example the Luther Bible in the book of John use says 'das verlorene Kind' meaning the lost child: but the use in 2 Thessalonians 2:3 as 'das Kind des Verderbens' means the child of corruption.[42]

So which is it? Why does it matter?
Judas did fulfill prophecy,

Psalm 49:1 *Even my close friend in whom I trusted, Who ate my bread, Has lifted up his heel against me.*
Proverbs 27:6 *Faithful are the wounds of a friend, But deceitful are the kisses of an enemy.*

---

42 https://en.wikipedia.org/wiki/Son_of_perdition.

Do we believe so great a sacrifice to cost Jesus His life might not have collateral damage? Is so complete a salvation incapable of redeeming one of His disciples that struggled with the corruption of his sin nature? He was a thief after all. Still, Christ called him, prayed for him, and told him to do what needed to take place for the arrest to continue Jesus's making a way for forgiveness. He even called him a friend as the betrayal was carried to its fulfillment.

> *"And Jesus said to him, 'Friend, do what you have come for.'*
> *Then they came and laid hands on Jesus and seized Him."*
> — Matthew 26:50

Oh, the angst that gives to consider how that might have undone Judas. We know nothing of his mind or soul. God does. We know God's word and it says in Proverbs 18:24 *"...But there is a friend who sticks closer than a brother."*

Only God can know Judas' heart and mind. We are limited to speculation and biased perspective by Judas' act of betrayal then his final act on earth. Do we opine and derive meaning about suicide erroneously when it comes to shrinking away from the subject? It seems so, and it has gone on far too long. Reader, this matters because as believers, we are stewards of all life. We will give an account of what we did and did not do. The compromise of a life is something we cannot sit by, hide from, or run away from as if the subject is too big to face. People are literally dying unaware of how to endure and persevere out of darkness and into God's healing and mending the soul.

Among the countless conversations I have had with survivors of an attempt to end their lives, it is not uncommon that many confess that death was not the result they really wanted, the pursuit was to stop the enormity of pain. That pain may be caused by emotional, mental, or physical situations, or any combination of those faculties of what makes us human. It is heartbreaking to know that pain can be so great that the mind can become clouded.

Count it a blessing if your soul has not sustained a moral injury,[43] for the pain of moral injury[44] rips at the soul.

Transition

What, then, is a "sober mind" versus what scripture commands and cautions? Why is it important? The full definition ascribed by Merriam-Webster may surprise the reader. The word "sober" as an adjective is descriptive of the condition of mind and its impact physically to a body. This begs the question: What about the human spirit? Again, scripture is clear as to what happens to the heart of one whose hope is deferred. The levels at which one can become heartsick have many pre-existing conditions and past tragedies with which to contend. Pre-existing conditions may include thoughts,

---

43 Moral injury occurs when an individual feels, thinks, or believes that "a transgression occurred and that they or someone else crossed a line with respect to their moral beliefs. Guilt, shame, disgust and anger are some of the hallmark reactions of moral injury (Farnsworth et al. 2014). Guilt involves feeling distress and remorse regarding the morally injurious event. Shame is when the belief about the event generalizes to the whole self (Norman et al. 2014).Disgust may occur as a response to memories of an act of perpetration, and anger may occur in response to a loss or feeling betrayed (Purcell et. al. 2016). Another hallmark reaction to moral injury is an inability to self-forgive, and consequently engaging in self-sabotaging behaviors."

"The attention that moral injury has received over the past decade shows that the concept resonates with individuals who have experienced a morally injurious event as well as with clinicians and researchers. A biopsychosociospiritual model has been recommended as a framework for obtaining the knowledge needed in order to understand and address moral injury in treatment." (Griffin et al. 2019).

44 Spiritual distress has been shown to be an important mediator between PTSD symptoms and moral injury (Evans et al. 2018). It may manifest as struggles with religious/spiritual communities, theological and moral principles, and one's relating to a higher power (Exline et al. 2014). Mounting research around spirituality and trauma-related issues suggests a critical link between spiritual distress and clinical outcomes for many survivors (Bryan et al. 2018; Currier et al. 2014, 2015a; Harris et al. 2008, 2012, 2018).

feelings, and possibly unhealed spiritual, psychological, emotional, or traumatic wounds. We don't only carry these things, but we must realize they impact us on the five levels of humanity: physical, emotional, psychological, spiritual, and expressed by behavior. Merriam-Webster includes the word "abstemious" as synonymous with sobriety. This is a comportment marked by restraint usually to food or drink. Additionally, abstemious behavior exercises restraint or by biblical principle, acts with self-control.

The biblical definition of "sober" is that of a mind fixed on Christ, able to operate with the Spirit of God in control and by passion for Christ, not emotions, in a moment, continuing to choose wisely and in a manner that glorifies God.

In scripture, the woman caught in adultery provides one of the most profound inarguable scenarios in which a person would carry feelings to include shame, embarrassment, fear, and utter humiliation. That she was an adulteress carried with it a stigma, not the likes of surviving an attempt to take one's life, but certainly, it can be agreed the situation was dire and only the presence of Christ redeemed her public shame.

A person should not be shamed for sin. We must do what is mandated of us: make disciples. That means we teach all that Jesus commanded. If suicide were not meant to be discussed in church, there would be no instance at all in scripture that demonstrates various causes and that *is* something that needs to be addressed.

This is a step in the right direction. Those impacted must speak up. Those restored must be strong and courageous to help others. We must be willing to ask and be ready to listen to the answers of those with priceless insight. Such knowledge should not be exclusive to therapy. It is Christ that restores; therefore, it must be His people who are available to pour out brotherly love as one journeys to thrive and become a victorious warrior for the Kingdom of God.

Those that grieve or who have lived experience with crisis are often willing to share insight as long and they feel safe in their vulnerability and know they can trust that there is authentic compassion and care for them.

Crisis will increase the closer we are to Christ's return, so let us be found expressing and serving in brotherly love like this: cherish life and go the distance with others. The cost was worth it to Christ, it should be worth it to us to save lives in as much as it is possible for us to do. In the remainder of this book, you will discover quite a lot about trends in ministry, both in leadership and from those with experience during their crisis.

May God bless you in staying the course of discovery. He knows for what purpose the truths of His word have been sent. With so much laid forth as foundational to improving how we, as a church, love others through the crisis of suicide, I would be remised not to include the importance of hindsight. The advantage of living years after written as is biblical accounts, or surviving and overcoming any crisis is hindsight. Uniquely today, we have the opportunity to read about fulfillment as many of God's promises have come to pass. Our hindsight advantage gives us hope similar yet different from people in the bible—contemporary challenges differ while applying God's timeless principles are consistent and relevant for today. Lived experience can impassion a calling and ignite a purpose beyond what one can see during life's storms. For that reason, the next layer in the foundation set forth will lead to the trends identified in today's culture ranging from ministry leaders and including the voices of those with lived experiences of various crises but with one thing in common; each survivor was impacted by suicide. Testimony is a mighty contributor to build any case. In this case, the purpose is to present compelling evidence so that you come away inspired to do your part to stop the neglect of ministry much needed to those impacted by suicide.

HINDSIGHT HELP

H istorically, tragedies lead to lessons learned. It is no different within the church. It should be no surprise we are offered repeated opportunities to consider how to minister during and in the wake of critical incidents in the program of eschatology. In times of devastation, be it a job loss, threatened economy, broken marriage, unseen health threat, sudden death, natural disaster, or terrorism—people need hope and help. It is reasonable to anticipate a greater need as frequency and escalating levels of impact touch more lives. Given that a Christian-worldview places faith in a sovereign, omnipotent, and omnipresent God, we must grow without compromise. It is essential to proactively evaluate the recent COVID-19 pandemic and how the church experienced major shifts in how ministry is done on account of the need for society to remain socially distant in church, work, and other areas of life.

HOPE DEFERRED

Is it contrary to offering hope when we do not face the uncomfortable areas of ministry that arise? How is it possible that the center of hope, the church, inadvertently turns away those most in need of hope, and help? What will the church do concerning stigmatized circumstances that are touching an increasing number of lives? Is the church ready to act on available information that is indicative of what may be on the horizon, presenting the need to rethink how we prepare for and do ministry?

The events of September 11, 2001, and how the world changed as a result of terrorism, was followed by many acts of heroism. The years since 2001 continue to provide lessons learned, particularly in how ministry leaders can better serve persons impacted by traumatic events when they ask for spiritual support. In introducing the concepts of *Stewardship of Wellness* and *Stewardship of Mind*, let it be established that we all have mental health. To what extent one is able to manage their health, that one's health is compromised, or that health is recovered comes down to their understanding of two biblical principles: that our bodies are fearfully and wonderfully made, and that one can be transformed by the renewing of the mind. From these two principles comes *Stewardship of Mind*, learning and developing what no one wants to lose and what few invest time to develop resilience to. Can you sustain or attain a mind capable of regaining self-control when all else may be chaotic? *Stewardship of Wellness* is similar but with the focus of growth and submission to what God is immeasurably able to do in and through us, even when conditions of mental health deal with stigmatized circumstances. Both concepts have to do with embracing our entire being—a mind, body, and soul—a miracle temple of the living God.

Today, we know that the levels of impact experienced on account of what happened on September 11 is associated with a person's proximity to ground zero. Similarly, following natural disasters, personal tragedies, and other acts of terrorism, including mass shootings and even deaths by suicide, society experiences a disturbing increase in compromised mental health caused by traumatic stress. In a study called *"A Ripple Effect"* conducted years after the World Trade Center was destroyed, it was found that friends, coworkers, clergy, and primary care physicians were most often the preferred source of a first line of support rather than mental health professionals. Although the subject of mental health continues to have breakthroughs in reducing stigmatization of the need for such, there is much room for improvement.

A lack of understanding how laity can participate as an effective part of the mental health continuum to sustain wellness requires the attention of leaders in ministry. Where ministry is concerned, theology and psychology are didactically compatible, still topics not taught in seminary or Bible college that are part of vocational and volunteer ministry need to be evaluated. The reason for the need to equip in these skills is that demand in the church and community have given rise to crisis response organizations that utilize chaplains and laity skilled in psychological first-aid and frontline triage care. Such ministry skills are imperative and align with ecclesiology (church theology) and eschatology (last things theology) on the level of our readiness to increase ministry as Christ's return draws nearer. While chaplaincy is considered pastoral care, it is unlike pulpit ministry. There are skills that it behooves a broader range of members in the church to gain for the purpose impacting more lives at a deeper level. It is time to utilize the equipped servants that deploy as an extension of ministries endorsed within the church. How much more would a distraught person find hope, if the one listening knew the value of being present and silent? How much more effective could ministry be if those ministering could ask good questions that can actually help others debrief from overwhelming situations to a place of initiating the *Stewardship of Wellness* and *Stewardship of Mind*? One need not be a licensed professional in order to contribute to the continuum of mental health.

It may seem odd to discuss crisis management and emergency preparedness as a consideration to strategize prioritization among church leadership. Both perspectives are needed given the role and identity of the church. End time prophecy is clear that circumstances will escalate and with them will come increased opportunities that require stretching beyond any comfort zone to meet people in very difficult situations. Traditionally church leadership has operated in a more reactionary manner than planning and preparing to respond to what trends and scripture indicate are inevitable. To respond is better stewardship and allocation resources by planning and preparing for the possible and operating in the probable. It is a different type of flexibility already found in ministries. Tragically, it could be that we have become so heavenly-minded that we are missing some of the earthly good that Kingdom-living should impact. If we learn anything from COVID's forcing the need for churches to pivot and minister outside the buildings, it should be that ministry needs to change in some practical ways without compromise to and in light of the message preached. There is hope.

PIVOT

The current pandemic did not come without advance knowledge and warning. Still, how unpredictable and widespread the impact would be was initially unknown. At the time of writing this book, a full insight of outcomes is yet to be realized. Nonetheless, it became obvious that stay-at-home orders resulted in a modern-day diaspora of the church leaving her brick and mortar place of congregation and having to minister differently. In the early few weeks, alongside the toilet paper panic, was a sudden spike in live stream services, web-based prayer meetings, and online small groups. It all happened at an almost maddening pace that seemed to challenge ministry-as-usual to a more intentional focus on staying connected with others. Due to physically congregating progressively coming to a halt, in one country after another the realization of what social distancing meant to pastoral ministry became a harsh reality. A shepherd and the many volunteers who serve were now unable to tend the sheep in the same way, causing quite an online frenzy. What did the experience feel like to you? What thoughts popped into and higher up in our minds as priorities? What observations were made? What lessons were or are still being learned? How did you pivot?

Using an acronym for P.I.V.O.T., I have included insight and lessons learned from the events surrounding the COVID-19 pandemic. First let us turn attention to the position and influence you have, as an individual or an organization. It is an important con-

siदेration when a sudden need to pivot is required to meet needs
and continue to provide service.

POSITION

For all practical purposes, as the coronavirus spread, the world
went into survival mode. As mentioned previously, in the phasic
progression of disaster, this is common. Congregations of all sizes
faced the involuntary need to minister differently. Some found the
position for progression to be less of a stretch because there already
existed an online ministry presence. For others with less presence
in digital space, the ministry faced challenges similar to those in
disaster. Interviews with numerous pastors and denominational
leaders affirmed a suspicion of ministry fatigue linked to common
denominators found in pastoral care leaders.

Churches who were more postured for digital ministry found
it an opportunity to come alongside smaller churches and congregations who were not as current, and utilizing live stream created
the need to make informed decisions about how ministry would
continue. The complexity included realistic evaluation of what was
best for each congregation. Not all services were best provided on
the world wide web. Congregants of high risk and shut-ins because
of age, disability, or not familiar with technology or that don't use
a computer had to be served differently. There was collaboration
in many cases.

IMAGINATION

The creativity of how the church and leaders went into action
was diverse and practical. Some met with challenges like drive-in
style worship that found opposition as a breach of how many could
safely gather within social distancing guidelines. Still, the imagina-
tive minds God placed in the church found expression by leading
the way as to how couples were married and how we celebrated, as
birthday and baby shower drive-bys were born!

VALIDATION

Repeatedly the church proved the need for a building while a place of gathering for worship would not be the end-all of taking ministry to communities at a whole new level.

One pastor set up a lawn chair with his own sign with a single powerful word: prayer! People responded! Congregation supported and took on the task of caring for frontline responders. Some have realized the needs I present in this work, that there is some readiness but not near enough readiness for the aftermath to come. Heroes will become burned out. They will realize their vulnerability. And prayerfully they will turn to the church. We need to be prepared to allow them to defuse, be heard, be validated for how real their experiences are, and meet them with a ministry of presence that may at times not require more than being available in their pain or fatigue.

OPPORTUNITIES

The plethora of opportunities that continue to come have not been exhausted. What is evident is the church has learned it will make permanent and long-term changes because of what she has learned about her reach. How many and how people are ministered to has and will continue to change.

During the writing to this book, the increase of those asking for help confirmed the needs expressed in these pages. There will be expanding opportunities to be creative and positioned to make a greater kingdom impact. Crises are not all bad, from them as He always has, God works things together for good and his glory.

TRANSFORMATION

Considerations for ministry include evaluating current reality. Then think ahead, anticipate residual impact to individuals and the community, both congregational and locally. The problem is that how to minister following a personal crisis or disaster are rare, if found at all, in seminary syllabi. It is little wonder why so many people with expectations and hope of a church leader's capabilities depart the church hurt, disappointed, or referred to care providers who are unable to provide pastoral care. So, what is the answer? What are some viable solutions to meet such practical needs?

Pastors do their best and are only human. Vocationally speaking, pastoral roles demand more than is humanly reasonable to expect. Members are parts of the church body to whom many will turn to as the first line of inquiry and care by individuals traumatized or in crisis. This necessitates we equip members in stewardship of mind, body, and soul. It is time that the church assesses pastoral care and equips the saints for the inevitable. Christ will return, and until then, the world will remain corrupt, hurt, and searching for hope. Hope is affirmed when those searching encounter help. Meeting the most basic need opens the door to minister and often that may be at life's most vulnerable moments. How now shall we love one another?

The number of physical injuries during and after a crisis is a minimum of forty percent higher when victims of post-traumatic injuries or stress associated with the event are included in incident impact. Invisible wounds are those that may be disclosed in conversation among a small group, close friends, coworker, and clergy long before considering seeking help from mental health professionals. It is at this level that the church must step up discipleship and ministry. Often those invisibly wounded inevitably need or seek support within trusted relationships within a similar worldview. If it is true that hurt people hurt other people, then persons healed and transformed are vital to those in need of healing and recovery following traumatically stressful events. When mitigated, such care initiates the beginning of the continuum of keeping a sober mind versus a compromise to one's overall health, including mental and spiritual health. This is *Stewardship of Mind*. It is time for ministers to aptly meet people in need of hope and help by modeling the *Stewardship of Wellness*.

By and large, the span of crisis response in the church is non-existent. Ministers have many imposed expectations, of which many are unreasonable or attainable. A recent study coupled with current events has given a rise in awareness of a gap of preparedness. The fact is that none of us know precisely how end times will unfold. Leadership must evaluate how we pivot from a systematic brick and mortar ministry and step up to equip congregants better to meet the needs of expectant seekers in the hope that the church can walk with them through their crisis.

Bright Future

Leadership has at hand a pivotal opportunity to reach all nations in ways not previously utilized. Knowing all that is at hand and at stake, it is a time of transition and transformation. We must grow and learn from history, and with a freshness and zeal for such a time as this.

God's people must lean into service and then serve abundantly. It is my hope that the seeds of perspective planted here become seedling work that flourishes, and I believe it will according to who God is and that He is able to do exceedingly and abundantly more than we ask or imagine. When we use hindsight to look into the future, we can see things differently. Crisis ministry has been around since the fall of man, may it be that ministering to all manner of crises redeems many a man, woman, and child. There is hope!

Introduction to the Study

The church, its leaders, and members represent the believing body of Christ. As children of God, we should be available to traverse all life's seasons of suffering, even when trauma and suicide shatter the lives of our neighbors. The ministry of hope, help, and presence we provide is one that must be realized as being dramatically different than what the world has to offer.

Stigma, shame, fear, or any other challenge of the aftermath of tragic events should not interfere with the ministry of courageous availability. We must help others face modern-day giants such as the survival of abuses, deaths by suicide, homicide, and ministry to survivors of attempted suicide. Care, help, and recovery must not fall solely to the field of mental health; following a crisis, the whole soul is in need of transformation and healing.

This completed work comprises three distinct and different components. The goal and purpose of these three distinct sections are to present a problem, highlight biblical foundations to guide our solutions, and to provide a testimony that is intent on equipping others. Part One expounds on the discoveries found in a focused study. It presents research conducted to identify trends in ministry from three perspectives: pastoral leaders, chaplains, and stakeholders, or those who have survived traumatic events. Part Two points the reader to Scripture that specifically addresses the subject of suicide. Part Three, the final section, provides testimonials and lessons learned through the transformation and merciful guidance of God by the Holy Spirit.

I hope that the church arises to be the light so desperately needed in places of trauma and crisis. We are commissioned, empowered, and sent to pierce the darkness grief leaves behind in the wake of suicide and other tragedies. Without awareness and a shift in prevailing perspectives, each one touched by trauma is at risk of having his or her physical, emotional, and spiritual needs go unmet.

Science continuously proves the truths of Scripture. Shouldn't the Bible be the foundation by which a soul is restored following life-shattering incidents? Wellness of the mind, body, and spirit are a matter of stewardship and submission. The gift of transformation by the renewing of the mind originates with God. If we—Christians—are living in the spiritual boundaries of Scripture, upon which eternity is founded, then restoration for those in crisis must include spiritual healing. It is up to the ministers of Scripture to take the mantle and lead the way to God's mercy for our vulnerable neighbors in crisis.

PART ONE:
IDENTIFYING TRENDS

A Study to Identify the Current Situation Pertaining to the
Church's Response to Crisis

INTRODUCTION TO PART ONE

T oday more than ever, human beings are finding new ways to commit outrageous assaults on one another. Between technology and accessibility to weaponry, horrific events such as workplace violence, school shootings, and an alarming increase in death by suicide are escalating and seemingly more frequent, leaving behind survivors who hurt in ways they never thought possible. Natural disasters, although not initiated by ill-human intent, contribute to turmoil in communities as well. Suffice to say, in the face of these trends, it behooves ministry leaders to evaluate their preparedness in responding to life-altering events. The bombardment of pain can fatigue communities over long periods. The impact of invisible wounds on some individuals can continue to surface long after the initial event is over, creating a cycle in which hurt people hurt more people in various ways. The Center for Disease Control indicates that violent death, and specifically suicide, are creating a tsunami of persons traumatically bereaved.[45] This study, conducted among pastors, chaplains, and survivors of traumatic events, reveals genuine ministry needs. It is time to face how spirituality, religion, and church factor into this conflict and address the need for resolution. How does faith factor into a personal triumph? How do people surmount traumatic stress? What is church leadership doing to face these giants?

Awareness ignites the probability of change. Without it, ignorance prevents light from dispelling the pervading darkness.

---

45 https://www.cdc.gov/violenceprevention/suicide/index.html

Traumatic stress can commonly be compounded or aggravated by high exposure to media; be it social media or headline news. To be unaware can agitate an individual's hidden struggles or inner conflict and compounds the problems within communities. The general public is ill-equipped with useful resilience skills or techniques in personal stress management. For people of faith, specifically Christians, church leaders may naturally be the likely "go to" persons in the line of defense. Of course, depending on a faith community, one cannot assume that all spirituality is Christ-centered. In light of pluralism, crises of faith become a hotbed of vulnerability for individuals traumatically impacted by invisible wounds. Invisible wounds can be inflicted morally, spiritually, emotionally, or physically through traumatic injury. The increased number of volunteers stepping up to serve during traumatic events can subsequently result in another impact on church members. How so? Volunteers bear emotional burdens that they either carry alone or they cope with by withdrawing. This isolates them as they do not have access to relevant ministry resources for post-trauma stress or even general stress management from a Christian worldview. There is a marked difference in a counselor who is faith-based versus a counselor that happens to be a Christian, but is more inclined to be science-driven, while leaving biblical counsel to pastoral care. The bottom line is that no one can give what he does not have. A weary soul cannot authentically minister effectively to others when fighting a personal battle. Weary souls unknowingly are open to what can become catastrophic spiritual vulnerabilities.

Peace persists where a soul abides in the stewardship of the one mind, body, and soul one is called to care for as the temple of the Holy Spirit. When difficult life events are brought forth in hope and faith that church leaders can help, we *must* respond. Needs and expectations cannot go unmet without the result of some hurt. When an individual acting in faith seeks help from his church and is met with referral outside the body, or the help given is not consistent with his Spiritual core values, it can result in unrest and internal conflict that clash with belief and confidence of care.

This project presents three perspectives: church leaders, frontline chaplains, and those with lived experience. From them, we can learn how something done in the name of ministry can actually result in significant challenges for the person in need of help.

The study seeks to provide candid answers to questions from various perspectives as to the effectiveness of ministry, as perceived by people directly impacted by invisible wounds from traumatic events. It aims to provide strategy and viable solutions for how the church can improve its support to those affected by a personal or family crisis, a loved one in crisis, or following a death by suicide or suicide attempt. Intentional ministry to those in crisis must be able to prove helpful in the reconstruction of individual lives and within communities in the aftermath of trauma. As such, it must be asked: Do present beliefs and practices function to support growth beyond the critical incidents?

THE STUDY — STRUCTURE

STUDY PARTICIPANTS

Following institutional review and approval of the project, sixty individuals including church leaders, chaplains, and trauma survivors participated in the research by individual interview. The invitation to contribute was given by public notice on social media, through personal email requests, and by phone calls to assure equal and diverse representation that spans mainstream pastoral care leaders: specifically, pastors and chaplains without exclusion of leadership willing to participate. Participants also included members of the general public who were referred by others aware of the study to create a holistic study representative of current trends without bias.

The study includes community-based participatory research (CBPR) within the community of trauma and suicide stakeholders.[46] These participants shared valuable insight into what research has often failed to include as questions in the research topic of crisis response in ministry. A study of this nature would be incomplete without the guidance of those from the field and those with lived experience.

The purpose of this study is to present perspectives of current trends in ministry as seen by ministry leaders and the stakeholders. Results of this study could be used to give insight to those in ministry as to the effects of trauma and how the church might better meet people in their point of need. Furthermore, it is hoped that this will be a tool to effect change and growth within faith communities. No other research of this nature was discovered prior to this study.

Even though the raw number of participants in church ministry was higher than that of stakeholders, participation percentages from those invited were significantly lower among church leaders than they were among stakeholders. One hundred pastors and chaplains were invited by a targeted social media ad campaign, personal email invitations, and phone call invitations. Seventy-five responded with interest to contribute. Declines were not included in the findings. Those who expressed interest received three follow up communication pieces that included full disclosure of the study, consent, and anonymity forms. Those who expressed interest, but ultimately were not available to interview, received a final thank-you. Of the initial seventy-five, only twenty completed the survey. Why such a low number? The subject of suicide as a ministry of crisis response is an increasing problem in society and a challenge not often addressed in church. The church should be a leading influence on crisis response ministry needs. However, a disturbing trend surfaced. Initial responses to participate were reasonably good. The disclosure was clear about the subject matter, and while

---

46   Stakeholders are the people directly impacted by, or who have a vested
      interest in, something. In this case, these are the people directly affected
      by traumatic events. To reduce redundancy, in this document, these
      people may be referenced interchangeably with the term "survivor."

this researcher did get polite reasons for changes of mind, only thirteen pastors and seven chaplains out of the initial seventy-five ended up providing much-needed data. Ministers are responsible to conduct funeral services for those who die traumatically, including death by suicide. Did the subject matter impact participation? Moreover, does the subject remain an elephant in the ministry living room? The findings are forthcoming.

There were sixteen stakeholders invited to participate. Of those, eleven contributed. The response percentage for stakeholders was sixty-nine percent, compared to a concerning twenty-seven percent participation for ministry leaders (pastors and chaplains). Overall, the entire study composition is thirty-six percent stakeholders and sixty-five percent clergy.

PARTICIPANT DEMOGRAPHIC

Denominational affiliation of participants included Adventist, Anglican Church, Assembly of God, Catholic, Independent Baptist, Southern Baptist, Church of Christ, Episcopal, Methodist, Mennonite, and those identified as non-denomination.

Congregational populations ranged from fifty to more than eight thousand members and represented churches from eleven states: Arizona, Arkansas, California, Georgia, New Hampshire, Louisiana, Oklahoma, Maryland, Oregon, Texas, and Washington State.

STUDY DESIGN AND ANALYSIS

This study is necessitated by the scarcity of qualitative and experiential data on how church leadership and stakeholders perceive the effectiveness of ministry in the aftermath of traumatic events expressly, but not limited to, suicide. The adopted approach used both virtual and face-to-face interviews. Interviews were recorded and transcribed verbatim with permission to use statements under anonymity. The study was explorative with data presented from three perspectives: that of a paid church leader in a pastoral role, a lay leader in either a paid role or the professional role of chaplaincy, and stakeholders that included survivors of traumatic events, including attempted suicide.

The Grounded Theory,[47] is a constant comparison of data to identify relevant themes, similarities and differences in contrasting narratives of stakeholders and ministry leaders, was used to group categories of perspectives in order to identify consistencies and gaps in the effect of ministry in the lives of those affected by tragedies.

PURPOSE

The inevitable escalation of traumatic incidents will impact the church at the local level as time progresses. This study seeks to encourage ministry and church leadership to consider evaluation, preparation, and emergency planning *before* disaster strikes. It must not be purely reactionary. Readiness response is a matter of stewardship. It utilizes the gifts, abilities, and indisputable testimony of survivors to impact others in a similar plight. The fact that more denominational groups are stepping up to respond and minister in times of crisis and many churches are becoming better at church safety is good shepherding. However, this study takes crisis response to a closer level of intervention. It focuses on the residual effects of crisis—the healing and full restoration that is much-needed but goes unfulfilled for many survivors. As ministers of the gospel, it is the role of the church to be continually growing and adjusting. To achieve goals requires a broad view of how effective ministry is perceived. Numeric attendance or staff evaluation are only pieces of the evaluative puzzle. Feedback must include subjective perspectives from those impacted directly by the ministry of the local church. That kind of feedback could change lives at profound levels. Church leadership response could start a strong movement by its witness of boldly and courageously stepping up their reach

---

47 Galser, Barney, and Anselm L. Strauss. *The Discovery of The Grounded Theory: Strategies for Qualitative Research.* New York: Adeline de Gruyster. 1967.

to meet people in places of pain. The world needs hope, and the church must step up the ministry of help in times of trouble.

Pastoral care does not solely fall to pastoral ministry within the church. Laity, volunteer, or professional chaplains[48] are also commissioned to be an outreach force who step into the frontlines as a ministry of presence during peak impact times of displacement and transition, trauma, and loss. It behooves the body of believers to collaborate in one study that seeks to present evidence, strategies, and testimony of what God will do, given His people's availability.

PERSPECTIVES

Requirements to be qualified as a pastor or chaplain in this study included a theological degree and a church or denominational endorsement. From there, specialized training varied, with sixteen percent of pastors having specialized training in pastoral counseling. Chaplains had skills training in Critical Incident Stress Management (CISM) or Psychological First Aid, teen crisis counseling, disaster relief, suicide prevention, and had been trained in how to give a death notification.

Chaplaincy care, as provided by the chaplains in this study, provides a ministry of presence and connecting individuals to a home church, if the individual has an affiliation or is active in the church. When that was not the case, the chaplaincy ministry provides care and resource support through the workplace or institutional/organizational leadership under which chaplains served.

---

48 The pastoral care of chaplaincy ministers to a diversity of specialty fields of the parish like places of service including but not limited to: airport, correctional facility, corporate, hospitals, hospice, and military pastoral care. It is usual and customary that chaplains undergo required and specialized training above and beyond what church pastors have to lead a congregation. Training may include but not be limited to clinical pastoral education, interfaith ministry dynamics, crisis stress management, or psychological first aid training depending on the scope of service for the groups served.

Responses

Pastoral Policies

C oncerning pre-existing policy and procedure for emergency or crisis response, does the church have a clearly stated policy or procedure for how to handle a family in crisis? Ninety percent of pastoral respondents did not have anything in place. Of the ninety percent, one was currently putting a plan in place, and two others had given it consideration. Following the interview, sixty percent commented similarly that this line of questioning had brought awareness that these are considerations that may need attention.

The term clergy includes pastors and chaplains from here forward. Thirty percent, that is nine of thirty, in ministry roles were personally impacted by the loss of a loved one or had personally attempted or had thought of suicide at some point in their lives. Among those with personal experience, there is notable empathy and grace concerning theological conclusions about eternal matters and what Scripture says. Surprisingly the majority of clergy polled could identify one or two examples of suicide from Scripture. Noted was the betrayal of Judas Iscariot, and some also cited Samson's death. This came as little surprise given that ninety-six percent of participants, including stakeholders, attest to concerns that the topic of suicide remains taboo or is the proverbial elephant that is not addressed in the church to the end that it is a problem in society.

Unless one has lived experience, there seems to be little interest in the pursuit of facing this giant from a biblical perspective.

The outcome of this study, while conducted without bias, prompted a practical response to address the subject in light of Scripture to demystify the unspoken truth. Suicide is tip-toed around for any number of reasons. It must be faced, and the material in this inquiry and the teaching to follow is propelled by study findings and on account of personal experience as a stakeholder with lived experience.

When asked if clergy felt prepared to minister more extensively beyond funeral and requested bereavement care, responses ranged from feeling "minimally prepared" to "somewhat prepared," but indicated they preferred to "refer to someone with specialized skills," like counselors, and only two indicated they were confidently well-prepared to meet the needs of those entrusted to their care. Only thirteen percent have a list of resources compiled and readily available when needed. The rest address situations as they arise.

COMMUNITY CRISIS RESPONSE

Natural disasters such as Hurricane Katrina and Hurricane Harvey have mobilized new groups of volunteers willing to help their communities in crisis. How proactive are faith communities in advance planning to serve when disaster strikes? Seven percent of congregations represented among eleven states part of the study are prepared with a designated role and readiness plan to help in the event of a community or nearby community crisis. The rest had either "some awareness" or "no idea" what groups or denominational response teams they would call upon when the need should arise. One hundred percent of clergy interviewed attest that congregations "could be better equipped" and that there is a "significant need" to educate and train groups how they can respond to community and personal crises. Pastors expressed a consistent sentiment as follows.

Response Comments:

Oklahoma

"The church needs to be able to help. It is meaningful to have pastors and chaplains trained. The average Christian needs to have at least a base level of tools to draw from to minister when a neighbor or friend come home with the pink slip of dismissal without being discouraging. Or if a relative has a spouse pass away, or when a friend has a spouse walk out on them. People make the biggest difference in recovery. The average Christian has no idea what to do and is unprepared. So what happens when someone has a tragedy? The average Christian ignores it or walks away because they do not know what to say or do and therefore do nothing at all. The average Christians need a few tools to know what they can do and how to do it. They need to learn how to love someone well, without feeling like they need to go through training as a chaplain."

California

"The church has to look at this as an avenue to extend the grace of God in the community of God to come around - that is a unity that God desires, especially for those that are broken and hurting in the community."

Texas

"Every church member can be a biblical counselor. It is a matter of giving them tools so that they can counsel one another. Let them know that typically this is something you can use to minister to each other and others. That way they know a biblical way of how to handle the topic and to minister to somebody."

ASSURANCE OF ETERNITY RESPONSES

It is common for bereaved survivors of a loved one who has been tragically killed to ask why and to seek assurance of things eternal. Two questions that are predictably asked in instances of death by suicide are "Why did it happen?" and "What about [the loved one]'s eternity?" Survivors want assurance of a heavenly eternity. A surprising trend surfaced about theological responses to these questions. Of the answers given, the views and opinions were biblically founded on principles in keeping with one's doctrinal conviction. Educational level among clergy did not seem to factor into how sure, uncertain, or ambiguous leaders responded.

When respondents were asked how they address survivor questions such as these, responses were either ambiguous or quasi-biblical.

Ambiguous Responses:

"I leave it in the hands of God. A person that would do that [suicide] is there is something unaccountable, and I won't make a judgment on the afterlife."

"As far as what that goes with eternal destination, basically what was done answers it."

Quasi-biblical Responses:

These responses are classified as quasi-biblical because the facilitator of the research identified them as deficient in providing an apologetic response. Biblical proof of what is "thought or believed" will give a higher chance of allowing the Holy Spirit to work in the person through God's Words. Christian apologetics provide a reason for what is believed and defend Christianity against objections.

"Personally, I don't think that [suicide] condemns anyone to hell. It is not something God wants for us. I do feel that God calls us to die spiritually and what often happens is that the devil gets hold of that and perverts and convinces someone that we need to die physically."

"Mental health affects us all, especially those that go so far as to take their lives. It is hard to say that one's eternal life would be determined by that one act in life. I would talk about those that have Jesus Christ, have eternal life and reassurance of that."

"There is always something we don't know. Suicide is probably the minority. Especially if they have taken their life in this day and time. People are influenced by so many things, whether it be mental-break-down, psychotic break, medications that can detach mental faculties from their will. I reassure them that if they are a baptized Christian, they can have every assurance that God will keep His promises. I do not think suicide is clearly enough defined or explained to tell somebody that their loved one is not going to heaven."

"Death, whether by suicide or other means, does not change our Christ status. If someone is in Christ, then she is in Christ. If he is not, then he is not in Christ."

"I believe that salvation is not lost no matter what we do. As I understand Scripture, suicide is nothing but sin. It grieves God's heart. It is self-perpetuated homicide; it is a murder. God forgives those who take the life of others, so why wouldn't he forgive this?"

"I think there are only two suicides in the Bible: Judas Iscariot and Samson. I believe Samson we will see in heaven, and I don't believe we will see Judas, because of betraying Christ. However, I think it is evident that there is nothing that can separate a person neither life, not death from the love of Christ if they've been born again and are a believer. So if a believer commits suicide, I do not believe that they lose their salvation, and we will see them in heaven. Unfortunately, if they are not a believer, I do not believe we will see them there."

SUMMARY OF THEOLOGICAL TRENDS

People who seek answers in times of distress often grasp for comfort to ease the pain and turmoil grief brings. Scripture is clear that we are to always be prepared to give an answer for what is believed.[49] It came as quite a surprise that not one pastor or chaplain gave an answer with any biblical support. This is an area that

49 1 Peter 3:15 instructs that our answers should be gentle and given with respect.

leaders can note for self-evaluation. People who are not pointed to the Bible continue to search for answers and lack the hope and help Scripture provides. The questions will arise, and when we answer questions with Scripture, there is a promise. God guarantees that when He sends His Word forth, it will accomplish the purpose for which He sent it. The general public is best served when people are guided to biblical support. It gives the foundation of faith they need as they seek answers from pastoral care.

A CRY FOR HELP

Among each variation of participant questions, the responses to the following question culminated in a themed cry for help.

Question: *If you could see a change in the church concerning trauma or suicide after-action ministry, what would that look like?*

Responses:

"Get with someone that has been through this and ask questions. Find out what they did, what helped them."

"Do not keep it a taboo subject. Have whoever is a resource be available. It needs to be known if there is a group or meeting that can provide resources that is a viable resource. Make the information available so that individually or anonymously, the person can reach out. Now it is not spoken of or talked about. It is only spoken about post-event. If there could be more awareness, more information on prevention and resources available, I would love to see that change."

"Get involved at whatever level we have to. We need to let go of what is being embraced lately— [the belief that] is it rude to ask a question. We need to forego all of that. We need to seek, need to share, and be available. Even if someone says they do not want to talk about it. Of course, back off in the immediate, but do swing back around and *do a follow-up. It does not need to be ignored. We are growing more as a society of people that do not get involved, and we need to get involved."*

"Every time we hear about God and who we are in God, it rebuilds who we are. If I knew who I was in God instead of just replaying the same things and going to the same schools and doing the same things... if I knew how to have a relationship with God, I would probably be able to handle the situation better. Knowing that there is something stronger out there and not just easily giving up helps. Knowing how quickly kids and teens are growing up, I don't think the church is providing enough ministry to the youth compared to what they [youth] are dealing with or need to know how to deal with that didn't seem to be prevalent when we were kids and what we are being exposed to in the culture. Having depth to ministry when it comes to Bible teaching would be helpful to equip teens and parents. It is great to have age-attracting service and fun-looking facilities, but we need to be equipped more for the culture we and the kids face every day."

"Start with having a safe space or group where conversations among those living through those traumas can come together for prayer, support, and to be guided from Scripture how to move ahead. This could be a small group, recovery class, or a conference that introduces hope and teaches what is helpful to get through this. A number of people at our church are foster parents. When we think in terms of trauma and its impact on people, I want people on one hand to have a broader idea of how to just listen better. And how do you begin to give a Christian advice without being a Christian busybody? Know when to speak and not just come across with Christian platitudes. I'm not saying [people] do that knowingly, but that is sometimes the way or how it can be [perceived]. Some of the hard lessons I have had to learn is that change comes slowly. And one of the fascinating things is that all of the work and research on brain chemistry and how trauma impacts [shows] that it can be undone, but it is not as simple as flipping a switch."

VOICES OF STAKEHOLDERS

When it comes to ministry, the body of Christ is called to love one another. No voice communicates more profoundly than that of a stakeholder. Stakeholders are the people directly impacted or have a vested interest in something. In this case, these are the people directly affected by traumatic events. How the ministry is perceived, experienced, or lacking to stakeholders with an assumed hope can be useful when it comes to supporting them. Availability is imperative to awareness. It is incumbent on church leadership to take notice of what is working, and what needs attention for the sake of improvement.

The following responses represent the perspective of survivors of various critical incidents and traumatic events. The purpose of this content is to provide unique and powerful insight for consideration when evaluating a ministry's effectiveness.

Throughout the 1990s until 2003, I participated in surveys and research studies that monitored consumer habits ranging from their hobbies, family recreation time, faith affiliation and religious participation, shopping habits, why product choices were made, and a litany of other behaviors essential for business development and assessing target marketing. The importance and magnitude of being one voice and the kind of impact each view has stuck with me and often validated why giving voice to the silent is imperative if we are to improve as a society. Calculations were based on a one to one-thousand metric, meaning that one voice represented one thousand others of a specific demographic profile. Currently, technology monitors such data by use of cookie software files that cross many platforms. While this study is organic and has no particular metric upon which to base how many consenting adults took part in the research, they do represent a significant part of the population. I propose that the information is considered as a serious opportunity to make incredible strides in ministry impact, reaching the unchurched, and to better serve members of churches. The participants included survivors of sexual, spiritual, psychological, and physical abuses. Some participants had a loved one who died by suicide, and others had attempted suicide and survived. The context for a greater understanding of scenarios is established.

Question: Based on your situation and pain, what recommendations can you offer to those that serve in a ministry that should be considered for others in similar cases to you?

Responses:

Lost a parent to suicide when respondent was a teenager.

"Let people know that the amount of struggle with stigma does not have to be that way. When people at church allow open talk about suicide, it helps. Many people do not have the upbringing I had in a church-going family. If the unchurched go through something like this, it is encouraged to talk to a pastor. Because it happened as my senior year started, after graduation, I started using alcohol and later joined the military."

A suicide attempt survivor, unchurched at the time of the incident.

"There was not much support. It would be helpful if the situation is known about for someone to be available. If there is a ministry, do not wait for a survivor to contact you. Because I was not faith-based at the time, there was no chaplain or ministry that I felt I needed to go to. I drank and took pills to numb everything. If someone had reached out, I may have pushed them away but knowing there was someone there if I needed them might have made a difference in attempting to die multiple times."

A churched teen at the time of a parent's death by suicide.

"An area for improvement is to not keep suicide a taboo subject in church. Have a resource available and be sure it is known among volunteers, leaders, groups, and staff so that the individual can reach out anonymously."

Lost a spouse to death by suicide.

"I would have been open to any help available if it was not preachy. What I needed, with small children, was someone to help me know what to do next. We were not prepared to cremate or think about a funeral. I had no idea how many death certificates would be needed. I was asked questions about accounts and so many things I did not know to move ahead day by day. It was hard to breathe and even remember to eat, or if the children had eaten. My assumption was that clergy and churches deal with that all the time and might have that kind of helpful information available for someone that knows nothing about what is involved when someone dies. No one came. I would have welcomed any faith-based group; Catholic, Buddhist, Christian. I needed help and I had no one to guide me."

Question: Did you find ministry to be helpful?

Responses:

Survivor of multiple traumas including suicidal family member, sexual abuse, spiritual abuse, and desperation of no longer wanting to live, but non-suicidal.

"With the group I was affiliated with the ministry was not helpful. Everything was responded to as the need for forgiveness and prayer. The skill set to help someone with levels of trauma I had required outside help, and that was frowned upon. Being shamed, not feeling worthy and made to feel guilty about things done to me were not going to help the issue. I had to get out of the environment and had to find what would help; therapists, doctors, and a coach that were more supportive to help. I have since changed my mind and found a place that I can allow ministry into my situation for healing."

Single parent whose spouse died by suicide.

"I did go to a counselor and gave him three strikes. I had to go see a counselor or the kids would not have gone. That is when we made the rule that you try something three times, and if you get absolutely nothing out of it, then it is okay to let it go. If you find that you got

something, even the slightest little thing or that something resonated and gave you something to think about, then you keep going. But my greatest help was from my tribe of support."

First responder.

"I need someone that does what I do and walks what I walk to be able to counsel me through problems or sticking points I might have. It is very difficult for someone regardless of good intentions to help me through sticking points when they have not been through what I go through personally and professionally."

Question: What are any unmet expectations of spiritual support from the church community?

"I am a big fan of where I attend, but I believe that the singles group crowd is severely lacking in support. Again, depending on a person's needs, there may be a greater need for connection. There seems to be more focus on older singles in some respect than for the thirty to sixties that have never been married, are divorced, or may not have any kids. For younger ages there seems to be a heavy focus on ministering to families with kids more so than for those unmarried. I know not all churches can meet the needs of all people, but that is my observation. I wouldn't say that is a negative thing. I just think that I am in a different zone, that many churches cannot support. Some of it is because of the church culture, and as a culture, we don't know how to handle the large population of divorcees and meet their needs. It goes to a more significant issue, and that is when someone in leadership is going through a divorce, them being kicked out sends a strong message to the rest of us. So there is some hypocrisy in beliefs and what we actually put on as a ministry front. When that is there, it is going to ripple down to people like me, if that makes sense? As a society, we have not really embraced what we believed and are not authentic. We seem to have to put up a front, and that is not necessarily what goes on behind the scenes. When it is said we love people and we accept anyone and

everyone to our church, but behind the scenes, other things are going on, it sends a mixed message."

"There needs to be an understanding of what someone's pain is and what hurt has been caused so that it can be dealt with appropriately and not have a fear of discussing it. A lot of people keep things quiet because they think that once they share the situation, there may be rejection, shame, or they'll no longer accepted to participate because they have a grievance. Instead [we need to be] willing to look at it with a different eye. Being willing to consider what a person has experienced and what could have been done differently to minister more effectively is a start. Being willing to be there even if someone is inpatient, outpatient, incapable of doing everyday life things like eating. These are not a lack of faith, but it is something that support goes a long way. The whole body (of the church) support needs to be factored into what the entire person needs overall. A sole focus on the spiritual first may not realize and support tangible, physical, financial, emotional, basic life things that need attention to walk into the situation and be more effective in the spiritual areas for the person in so much pain."

Question: Was there any form of a ministry of presence available and would that have been helpful at the time?

"There was nothing of a presence or support of that kind available. Yes, I do think that kind of a support ministry and presence would have been helpful in not feeling so alone. I also think that goes back to a skillset; I do not think the church had."

Question: How did you find people responded upon learning about your tragedy?

Suicide attempt survivor.
"Short term, there was blame or focus on what I did wrong rather than look at the pain I had. Long term it has been more empathetic because I have been able to pull myself out of it. Now people comment

that they are sorry I went through what I did. My response is that it now helps me help others"

Survivor of a loved one that died by suicide.

"People kind of avoided conversation about what happened. It seemed like some of the ones I thought would be around more, stayed away. I felt avoided. People got awkward when I started to talk about that family member. No one at the church asked if there was anything I might need. That really has hurt. Of all places I should feel supported, I feel like no one wants to talk about or help me with this."

Lost a spouse to death by suicide.

"Frankly, I could have done without a service. We did a service for the kids and other people. I did not feel like "let's celebrate his life" because it is a life he chose to end. I am angry at the way he chose to end his life and we are all still dealing with it. I encouraged the kids to hug everyone at the service and listen if they have something to say because ninety percent of them were not related, we will never see or hear from them again, because that is how it happens. They go back to their lives. While we are still trying to remember to stay hydrated, get something to eat, and carry a hanky around with us, they will be gone. They will be sad, but they are going to go on living their lives. It does not mean they don't care and I understand that it is ok that they have to go back to their lives. Just take time to appreciate that they're being here as a way of support. There were a few people that stayed and never backed off. Talking to people was a challenge for me, but texting meant that I could respond when I responded. It has been over a year, and I still get texts that may be as simple as a heart, or that say I am thinking about you. For me, not wanting to sit and talk to people all the time, that was perfect."

Question: What meant most to you about a faith community after the crisis?

Survived a suicide attempt.

"It is great when someone asks how you are doing, and most give a polite response of doing fine. But when you knock on someone's door, and you linger a little longer, it encourages that person. That is how we reach people. That stuck with me. If they had never come to my home. I would not have had these people for the next 55 years of my life."

"I really believe that without what seems like minor experiences, I do not know when I would have accepted Christ. Whatever they did be it a loaf of bread, a pie, or whatever they brought else, it was out of generosity to do so. That changed a child on another level. It changed my life. Until you asked me these questions, I didn't even see the origin. That is powerful."

Spouse of a suicide attempt survivor.

"It surprises me that the people that have stuck around are not the ones I would have expected to. These people, no matter what goes on in this roller coaster of life, are not going anywhere. They are connected to me like glue and I to them because I know it could not have been easy for them, especially the first few months when no one knows what to say. The small handful of people that stuck by my side checked in on the kids and just made sure that we know that they are there - those are the rarest people in the world. They are part of our tribe, and that is something I will never ever forget. I will never let go of them because you don't find people like that very often. When we go to our support group and answer, Who do you have that you can call when you are having a rough day? How many people don't have somebody? For me to be able to say and know that it can be three in the morning, I have at least four people on the top of my mind that I can call. I know that even at three in the morning they will pick up the phone and be there. So many people don't have one person they can call. I feel lucky to have the people in my world that I do."

Question: What would you tell someone in your situation that helped you most?

Abuse survivor.

"Early on, they need to find ways to make the situation its correct size. Often when people are left alone with their pain, it grows. Then it grows into something that maybe it wasn't. When we feed our pain over periods, it becomes bigger than the initial hurt. We need to go back and get honest about what happened and how that made us feel at the time, not overtime. We need to forgive sincerely and quickly. I believe that when we go back and revisit the original hurt even if it has been 20 years or more and if we are honest with ourselves about the original hurt, then we need to forgive those who hurt us. That forgiveness will be the kick start of the healing process. I believe that over periods, things that go unaddressed manifest into something way bigger. We need to bring hurt down to size."

Question: Is there any additional feedback that people and leaders in churches should know about?

"Get involved at whatever level we have to. Also, be aware of what the person to who you are ministering or that comes for some form of ministry support says and may not say. We need to let go of what is being embraced lately - that something is too rude to ask. We need to forego all of that we need to seek. Share and be available. Even if someone says they do not want to talk about it. Of course, back off in the immediate aftermath, but do swing back around and do follow up. It does not need to be ignored. We are growing more like a society of people that do not get involved, and we need to get involved."

OBSERVATION

A cry for help occurs when there is a need for intervention on some level. This study is not exhaustive, and participants represented a broad range of survivors of traumatic events. Suicide attempts impact a large part of the population, at an estimated rate of more than forty-five thousand in 2018, with statistics indicating that there are thirty attempts to every known and reported death by suicide.[50] Based on this, in the United States alone, we can know that over 1,364,000, families have survived and may be dealing with nightmare situations. Many of those people are members of churches and are either suffering in silence or have limited available ministry. The enemy would like nothing more than to have them leave the fellowship because no one ever asked, reached out, or offered ministry specific to their situation.

The study repeatedly indicated from various perspectives that the change needed is known, and the desire to resolve the problem is now documented. What remains is collaboration to meet people in places of pain and penetrate wounded hearts with hope and help from scripture and to provide skills to start the conversations few have allowed to be dealt with at church.

STUDY SUMMARY

Trends evident and highlighted from the data collected were not limited to, but did include, some discrepancy between leadership, congregants, and non-church attending interview participants with lived experience. Differences in perspectives are a common occurrence when roles and expectations differ from leaders to members. Surprisingly, and vocalized by survivors, the need to be pointed to scripture and the contrasting lack of biblical support from clergy were frequent concerns among survivors. Expressed was the need, hope, and expectation that a pastor or someone in ministry is able and available to provide biblical support in times of trouble.

The study provides measurable data and represents churches that span all regions of the United States. Denominational participation among a wide range of church affiliation dispels bias. A disappointing outcome that bears mentioning since it occurred multiple times with similar demographic sized mega-churches is that a good web presence and a contact us form on websites were

50 According to The Center for Disease Control and World Health Organizations.

delayed in response or not responded to at all. This can lead to disappointment for those in crisis or grieved who never heard back. Technology may actually limit a personal connection in a time of need.

On the five occasions that this was evident, I learned that some procedures place a high expectation on the person in need of ministry to ask for and wait for someone qualified to get back to them. In some cases, follow up never occurred. In others, follow-up consisted of an automated email letting me know someone would reach out in a few days. No one ever did. Sometimes in grief, a person may not have the emotional clarity and bandwidth to communicate a need. When bereaved, if a person should not have to muster the courage to reach out and then have the energy to reach out again and again while suffering in the pain of grief. Immediate follow-up is a necessity. Grief is time sensitive.

Finally, the study produced valuable data from which growth can occur. Subsequent sections of this project provide apologetic biblical and testimonial support to guide the church as to what can be done, how it is possible, and provide a helpful compilation of scripture support for addressing the topic of ministering to those touched by suicide.

PART TWO:
SCRIPTURE AND SUICIDE

BIBLICAL GUIDANCE

"Can you listen as if you might be wrong?" – Debjani Beswas

The words of Debjani Beswas during a 2018 TEDx presentation struck a chord. When considering the topic of faith, the Holy Bible, and Almighty God, his question is pertinent to ask. We ought to be willing to listen, but to whom we listen is imperative to consider. We listen in order to grow more intimate with all God is and wants to be in us and to us. It is personal. One challenge is that many do not believe a triune God exists. For some who do believe, it is a struggle to overcome the fact that God can and will communicate the same today as He did yesterday and will communicate tomorrow by His Holy Spirit. He is Father, Son, and Holy Spirit. The Holy Spirit remains true to who He is in the fullness of one mission: to reconcile the world back to how it was created by Father, Son, and Holy Spirit. Not three different gods, but a single, triune God in three persons.

"Can you listen as if you might be wrong?" Moreover, can you accept a message regardless of the messenger? What scripture does not say is as important as what it does say. When scripture is silent on a particular point, it is not wise to make a theological point. Such a point lacks biblical support. A biblical principle aligns with God's nature, word, and changing truth. The following will pose a challenge for you to consider where you are right now and how you feel about face a giant not openly spoken of in many congregations, even when death by suicide hits home.

During the research and interview phase of this study, respondents were asked: "Does the Bible address suicide?" All pastors and chaplains mentioned Judas. Some brought up Samson's death, not as a blatant suicide but a sacrificial death that could be interpreted as suicide. Only a couple included the incidents of King Saul and his armor-bearer as relating to a death by suicide. Of all the participants, only two mentioned they thought there might be more occurrences of suicide, but they were not certain. Only one referenced that there are seven deaths by suicide in the Bible. The seven deaths by suicide include Samson, King Saul, King Saul's armor-bearer, Ahithophel, King Abimelech, Zimri, and Judas Iscariot.

Inclusive of those suicides, there are numerous biblical references to people who had thoughts of wanting to die or be dead. Today such remarks would be considered suicidal ideation. Those who expressed such thoughts include Job, Elijah, Jeremiah, Jonah, and Paul. The Philippian jailor sought to take his life and was set to act rashly when the first and only mention of human intervention appears in scripture.

One of the biggest questions after a death by suicide is "Why?" Just as important is asking yourself is "How?" As in, "How will the fatality at hand make a difference for the living, beyond the tragedy?"

When a person dies by suicide, pain and grief are transferred and multiply as many times over as there are those grieving the loved one. To ask why is natural. To ask how plants an intentional seed and sparks human nature's need to beget answers. To ask how creates a better possibility of ministering with the intent to point people to coping solutions according to Scripture, rather than remain helpless with the ruminating of the why question. Only the person who is deceased and God could fully know that answer. It is my hope this section will challenge you to become a difference-maker.

What comes to mind at the mention of Judas Iscariot? Take a moment to jot down your current thoughts and beliefs. What does scripture say? Some doctrinal tenants have held that death by suicide made burial in Christian cemeteries impermissible and such internment was unorthodox. This was the case in the early church and continued within Catholicism until recently.[51] As we take a candid look at what the Bible does and does not say, ask yourself if you can listen to scripture as if you might be wrong. My desire is that we hear from and listen to Our Father.

Over the years, I have done my share of spelunking. I most frequently visit Carlsbad Caverns in New Mexico. One of my favorite moments is when all the lights are turned off, and the cave becomes pitch black. Each time I marvel from a different perspective: older and more learned. That experience mimics for me a life lived in a dark pit. The dark is so dense that the spark of a single match illuminates everything. Only seconds before, no matter how I strained my eyes, I could see nothing—not even the palm of my hand in front of my face. The match, however, brings vision with its light. Equally incredible was how blinding the lights were once fully turned back on. Complete illumination!

Death by suicide is complicated. Circumstances are challenging to navigate for survivors. Naturally, the struggle to find meaning or seek answers is met with so many opinions that lack biblical support. Arriving at conclusions surrounding death by suicide can vary. Tragically suicide is such an unhealthy common occurrence that the majority of people know someone who has died or attempted suicide and survived. The very act is one of a

---

51 Since the 1960s parishioners that died by suicide were permitted to receive a Catholic funeral and be buried in Catholic cemeteries. In the 1990s, during the tenure of Pope John Paul II and for the first time, the Catechism of the Catholic Church declared that "Grave psychological disturbances, anguish, or grave fear of hardship, suffering, or torture can diminish the responsibility of the one committing suicide."

The Catechism teaches: "We should not despair of the eternal salvation of persons who have taken their own lives. By ways known to him alone, God can provide the opportunity for salutary repentance. The Church prays for persons who have taken their own lives" (No. 2283). For this reason the Church no longer forbids funeral rites or burial to Catholics who have committed suicide. http://www.vatican.va/archive/ccc_css/archive/catechism/p3s2c2a5.htm

hurt person, who transfers that hurt to others. Suicide is a health crisis, according to the Center for Disease Control and the World Health Organization.

Judas betrayed Christ in exchange for thirty pieces of silver. Following his act, he died by suicide. What does the Bible say about such a tragic death?

The following passages and biblical principles should compel each of us to go to the Lord for answers. The intent here is to challenge every presupposition held to encourage us to listen to the help of the Holy Spirit to realize what scripture indicates surrounding suicide.

ACTIVATING MINISTRY

Scripture does not condone suicide, but it does speak about it and offers direct principles for how to activate ministry in such cases. Is the church ready and willing to boldly offer straight ministry to those who have been broken by such highly difficult bereavement? Some of what it reveals is the help needed by many to be able to take off the graveclothes of stigma, shame, fear, and find hope for healing in mercy and grace.

Scripture validates itself and the attributes of God. It does not contradict, so pay close attention. Prophetic scriptures surrounding the death of Christ are many and among them is the near and far fulfillment of Zechariah 11:12-13

> *I said to them, "If it is good in your sight, give me my wages; but if not, never mind!" So they weighed out thirty shekels of silver as my wages. Then the Lord said to me, "Throw it to the potter, that magnificent price at which I was valued by them." So I took the thirty shekels of silver and threw them to the potter in the house of the Lord.*

LESSONS FROM JUDAS

Judas was paid the same wages for the value placed on Christ. Now a close look at the betrayal as found in Matthew 26:24-25.

> *"The Son of Man is to go, just as it is written of Him; but woe to that man by whom the Son of Man is betrayed! It would have been good for that man if he had not been born." And Judas, who was betraying Him, said, "Surely it is not I, Rabbi?" Jesus said to him, "You have said it yourself."*

What Judas said that Jesus references at the end of this verse is not explicitly stated. Judas had earlier made arrangements to carry out the betrayal, and Jesus knew it in detail. This was part of the mission fulfillment of Christ's coming to demolish the wages of sin and to render mankind forgiven and freed of the death penalty due by the Law. Individually the call remains to come to Christ in repentance.

Let's consider what Jesus may have referred to when he said to Judas, "You have said it yourself."[52] Judas knew what was pre-arranged. Only God could have known what was said by Judas at some point. We don't know if he said it aloud or silently to himself. But we must wrestle with what scripture says and indicates. What is unseen by man is within the Omniscience of God, and that is the identity of Jesus Christ. Perhaps there was a battle raging in a man about to betray a friend. Matthew tells us that each was grieved. Mark tells us "they" began to be grieved. Luke, the doctor, wrote of the impending woe to that man by whom Jesus would be betrayed. As a physician, Luke would have had insight in what kind of woe and toll such betrayal could have on a body. John 13:21 includes the impact that telling the disciples had on Jesus. He became troubled in spirit as the disciples were at a loss to which one among them it would be.

Have you ever done something with a limited insight only to discover later that the choice made resulted in an outcome that led to regret? I once stole a piece of candy from a store *after* a parade that richly blessed me with a bag full of candy! The candy in the bag I received was not what I wanted. To my sincere regret and shame, I made it to the car, unaware of what might happen if I got caught. Honestly, as a five-year-old, I think I was trying to destroy

52 Matthew 26:14-15

the evidence before anyone could know what I did. In the back seat of the car I unwrapped the full-sized candy bar I craved. The wrapper betrayed me! The noisy paper sold me out and the jig was up. I was busted. I would rather have gotten a spanking than to be taken back into the store to tell the cashier what I had done. It was horrible. The vivid scene haunts me as I tell you what the unseen torment of guilt does when conviction overcomes a soul. Tears could not save me. I could not look at the one I had offended, and I remember shaking to the point of wetting my pants. Guilt impacts the entire mind, body, and soul.

Judas was among the grieved when Jesus said He [Jesus] was to be betrayed.[53] While there is no mention that Judas may have had an inner battle stirring, since he responded like the others, he dipped into the cup, and we know as did that Jesus spoke directly to him. Still, the outcome of Judas's pending betrayal was not fully realized at that moment.

By saying, "You have said it yourself." Jesus reveals to Judas something on which scripture does not elaborate. It is common to have many feelings when betrayal breaches a relationship. At best we know Judas was grieved. But Proverbs presents insight that must not be ignored: "A stone is heavy and the sand weighty, But the provocation of a fool is heavier than both of them."[54]

Nothing leaves a soul vexed like grief or guilt. The proverb goes on to detail quite a toll emotions and conflict can take that is unseen to others but known only to the one within whom a storm rages. "To be vexed" is strong language for many strong emotions. Anger has a root of pain at its core, and while scripture presents that anger is common, it instructs that we not sin in our anger. I don't know about you, but I have had such rage that it pained me all over, and outwardly manifested as hostile anger. The enemy taunts with accusations, abuse, and emotional chaos that can deteriorate the clearest mind. Wisdom of the same proverb tells us when someone is in chaos, clarity is diminished by self-talk. Projecting or to speak

---

53   Matthew 26:21
54   Proverbs 27:3

aloud allows the brain to release toxic hormones that overload to the point that a person can react in a state of fight or flight.

"Better is open rebuke than love that is concealed."[55] Judas returned the money, but to face the other eleven after three years of following Christ put Judas in a volatile moment of nearsighted torment. The devil had entered him, and what resulted may have led to what Proverbs teaches. "Faithful are the wounds of a friend, but deceitful are the kisses of an enemy."[56] Judas was both; friend and the one who betrayed a friend as an enemy. It does not end there.

Pay close attention to the behavior and language of scripture and ask yourself once more: "Can I listen as if I may be wrong about something I have held firmly to without asking the Lord?" By design, Judas led the arresting soldiers and identified Christ. Is betrayal unpardonable? Could betrayal possibly lead to guilt manifesting in behavior that indicates something we cannot know—condition or contrition? Judas reacted in remorse, radically uncharacteristic of a mere thief. He returned the silver to the temple, according to scripture,[57] and subsequently it was used to buy the Potter's Field, which was a burial place for foreigners. After all that, it came to be called the Field of Blood since that was where Judas took his own life.[58]

IRONY OR ILLUMINATION?

There must have been a mad scramble when the betrayer came to the temple, confessed his sin, which by the standard of the Law demanded a life for a life. What did the chief priest do? They did not care. Moreover, Judas is told what he already knows: "That's your responsibility." There is very little worse than admitting you're wrong and being helpless to reverse the damage one's actions caused. The reaction tells us more than we ought to conclude. His behavior indicates remorse. He confessed guilt, returned his pay, and was

---

55 Proverbs 27:5
56 Proverbs 27:6
57 Zechariah 11:12-13
58 Matthew 27:5, Acts 1:18

rejected by those responsible for spiritual restoration according to the Law. Like many in a state of desperation, nearsighted pain, guilt, and inexplicable chaotic turmoil, Judas took matters into his own hands before he could ever know that the One able to forgive was yet to die and rise again. Atonement for sin had not yet been completed and grace was not a concept yet understood or revealed as a probability according to the Law. Since God overlooks sin in our ignorance,[59] can anyone really know that Judas and his act of betrayal is the precedent upon which religions and many people have concluded condemnation when someone dies by suicide? We know the devil entered him. We do not know if he also left him at some point. Behavior indicates a shift in motive. Typically, a thief keeps what is stolen or what is ill-gotten gain. Judas knew the Law, and after three years with Jesus there was some connection. He seemed to act in accordance to the Law's demand for restitution.[60]

Blood money was thrown into the temple, that was contemptible, but did the Chief Priests take any responsibility? No. They bought a field and credited it to Judas purchasing it, when Matthew is clear what happened after he threw the money in the temple. He hanged himself. How then according to Acts 1:18 or Matthew 27:5-10 could Judas have purchased the field for foreigner's burial? Can a dead man purchase land?

Note where the tragedy ends—in a field for foreigners. Betrayal can leave the guilty feeling so estranged from the one he betrayed. How have we arrived to conclude that it is certain where Judas spends eternity? Perhaps something critical in Acts 1:24-26 has both eluded us and in our own error left us to assume we know where Judas belongs. Do not miss some key points Peter made about scripture fulfillment. As the apostles prayed for Judas's replacement, there is a paradox when they pray, "Lord, you know everyone's heart." It is the same language of Proverbs 27 that speaks of wounds of a faithful friend. Did he act only as an enemy or does scripture possibly reveal something we may have never considered

---

59   Acts 17:30
60   Exodus 22:3

about Judas and God's grace, mercy, and predestination. Prior to the passion of Christ, only King David had declared that God knows our days before one of them comes to pass. Inspired by the Holy Spirit, Paul teaches about predestination. Only God knows the heart.

Continuing with Judas, we must deal with what Mark and Luke tell us concerning forgiveness and what exactly is unpardonable. "Truly I tell you, people can be forgiven all their sins and every slander they utter, but whoever blasphemes against the Holy Spirit will never be forgiven; they are guilty of an eternal sin."[61] All means all. There is only one exception. One could argue that by actions leading to suicide Judas did not blaspheme. The biblical definition as found in Matthew 12:30-32.

"Whoever is not with me is against me, and whoever does not gather with me scatters. And so I tell you, any sin and blasphemy can be forgiven. But blasphemy against the Spirit will not be forgiven."

By his actions, according to scripture: Judas was seized with remorse, he returned to the temple, gave back the money, confessed his wrong, and acknowledged the innocence of Christ. Al behaviors suspicious of a penitent individual. God alone knows the heart of a man, while he did take his life and acted in contempt of his Creator, biblical evidence strongly suggests that a thief is suspect of what we cannot accurately judge. Perhaps what we judge from a place of never having been at a place of such desperation has more to the story by means of hope for those grieving the loss of a loved on to suicide. blaspheme. This is perhaps one of the most challenging things to reckon when it comes to thinking about the "elected." It is a hard teaching, but some are set apart for noble purposes and others for ignoble purposes, and still in all things, God works for the good of those who love him and who have been called according to His purpose. Jesus's death had to fulfill scripture.

To summarize, I will leave us with some intentional questions. Truly the Lord wants to reach people in dark places to reveal hope.

---

61 Mark 3:28

He came to seek what is lost. What about Judas's behavior was unpardonable? Indeed, the enemy had entered him at least to the point of influencing his behavior, but in all that took place, did anything happen to be suspect of a desperately wicked heart that only God can know? The devil's method of operation is to prowl, kill, steal, and destroy. Suicide is the death of a vision, a hope for a future that will not be realized. It steals from survivors' future hope of a longing to live a long life here on Earth with those you love. For those who have ever attempted suicide and survived, know that the enemy seeks to steal peace, taint faith, and constantly attack one's identity. Suicide kills more than the life that acts to die by suicide. When someone survives an attempt, it ruins relationships. We are made for fellowship. It destroys trust. We are commanded to trust in the Lord and lean not on our own understanding. That is hard enough to do without complicating matters.

Someone in distress is vulnerable. The enemy is a liar and an accuser. He can use self-evident truths to insult injury, just like he did with the guilt Judas confessed when he went to his synagogue leaders. Could rejection in a time of desperation from those one thinks is the best resource for help or support be devastating? Yes; especially when one turns to spiritual leaders for some form of resolve that can only come from God. Therefore, it is imperative that we take to task the assault heaped on by the devil when it comes to desperation and suicide. The truth is that God's grace is greater than sin.

Is it possible that within the attribute of mercy and holy sufficiency to forgive all but one select sin, Judas's sin was no worse than what is written in the Law? I praise the Lord that Jesus has fulfilled the keeping of the Law when He laid down his life to pay a debt we all owe in exchange of a life we cannot ever purchase of our own merit. For the life of the flesh is in the blood, and the Lord gave Himself as full atonement for all who believe that Jesus Christ is the Lord and follow Him accordingly.

The problem of getting caught up in the challenge of reconciling a death by suicide is that only God ever knows the condition of a man's soul. Furthermore, the survivors grapple for answers that may never come to satisfy the need to know what went so wrong? The answer to "what went wrong" started way back in the garden of Eden. Subtle deception and a slight twist of what God said (and did not say) resulted in broken fellowship between God and His creation. There has been a war for the souls of men ever since.

The heart is deceitful and only God can know it.[62] A sick heart can manifest behavior that is out of character. As such we need to remember not to lean on our own understanding but to acknowledge God and come face to face with the fact that we have limits to what we can know.

To conclude this section about Judas, ask the Lord for peace regarding how He wants to grow you through whatever may be your greatest struggle on this topic. Can you consider that Christ came to forgive all sin, even self-inflicted death such as this? Ask Him to help you be bold and compassionate to those impacted by such tragedy. Ask Him to help your mind, attitudes, and language surrounding death, as it is so full of opportunities to minister to the broken and crushed in spirit. My prayer for you is that with help from the Holy Spirit, you and I will become more compassionate.

---

62 Jeremiah 7:9

Addressing Suicide

How Does Scripture Address Suicide?

It is a known problem that suicide remains a proverbial elephant in the room within the church and people in need, so what will it take to storm the gates of the enemy's domain? Deception, stigma, shame, a lack of skill, and neglect of ministry is costing lives and leaving casualties of war hurting in the pews. People leave our church doors without realizing the hope and help that exists among many silent believers. Lived experience and triumphant testimonies could make a marked difference in salvation and the saving of lives.

The church is called to rescue the perishing, and that is not limited to evangelism. There are models and principles throughout scripture to bridge the gap between the known need discovered and the cry for help of each participant involved in this project. Believers are called to lift the countenance of one another, and there are many principles that can be gleaned as we navigate the rough waters of the suicide tsunami. This kind of death is preventable.

The narrative of Jesus raising Lazarus from the grave is a good model by principle of how each believer has a role in restorative ministry. Every born-again believer is the dead man raised to new life. He was alive yet bound "by graveclothes." Graveclothes will be used here to represent sin. He was saved by grace yet bound by sin; he would die one day again. Lazarus stood at the opening of the tomb alive, yet Jesus told those gathered that they were to remove from Lazarus the graveclothes. Until others got involved, he was limited in ability to navigate in freedom or to testify to the glory of God. Collaborative ministry and first-hand accounts are potent testimonies, the likes of which silence the lies.

Martha was concerned with the potential for odor before the stone was rolled away. Imagine for a moment you are there. What might go through your mind when Jesus tells you to remove those rags? Let me help. "Oh Lord, you want me to remove oil- and herb-saturated, dried up, crusty clothes from a recently dead man? What will people say? I won't be able to worship at the temple the next Sabbath. Oh, and that one in the back dangling low, surely you don't want me to do that. That alone would make me unclean!" We can picture the visual, however, it is not much different when it comes to ministering to people in remarkably devastating emotionally dirty situations.

Adam and Eve faced trauma. One son murdered the other. The murderer became a fugitive. They lost two sons as the result of one tragedy. How did they handle it? There is not much detail, but it is certain that they came together. From that union came their son Seth. If you've ever known the heartache of losing a child, you know that it changes people. It strains a marriage. It is one of the rawest places of grief and pain a couple can face. Although they are one, each grieves differently. Each bears great individual grief, the likes of which the other cannot know. Yet they as a couple are one. Everything hurts. The first family in the Bible dealt with trauma and sudden loss.

The enemy will stop at nothing to destroy the church and its people. Therefore, the church must lead the charge to confront our enemy on God's terms for the damage of stigma, shame, and the need for souls to heal concerning identity in Christ and the authority believers have to destroy strongholds. Lives are at stake, as are the souls of those grasping for hope and help. Scripture has much to be drawn from to address the crises of our time. Ecclesiastes teaches that wisdom is greater than strength. The enemy may be crafty, but those with God are endowed with wisdom.

SIX MORE

As with any precept originating from God, scripture will not contradict who God is. Five of the remaining six suicides also mentioned in the Bible were acts of desperation to save face or avoid captivity and torture. The embarrassment and humiliation to have been remembered as a leader of armies who was killed by a woman was inconceivable for a proud man. Fear of torture and captivity under rules of engagement in war was another reason. Samson's was the only suicide that seems not to be reactionary in the same way at the others. While it was a decision, Samson's desire for retaliation for the loss of his eyes cost him his life. As he gave up his life, the Philistines were killed along with Samson.

GOD'S HEART ABOUT SUICIDE

God loves you and every one of His created beings. Suicide breaks God's heart.

Refer to this list for biblical support.

- Suicide rejects God's offer of inner peace that will guard the heart and mind. (Philippians 4:6-7)
- Suicide usurps God's sovereignty over the length of life He has planned to prosper and not harm you. (Psalm 139:13, 16)
- Suicide rejects God's desire to be Lord over you during a bad storm of life. (1 Corinthians 6:19)
- Suicide goes against the commandment not to murder. (Deuteronomy 5:17)
- Suicide denies God's ability to heal hurts. (Jeremiah 17:14)
- Suicide shuns His provision of hope and rest. (Psalm 62:5)
- Suicide rejects or overrides God's power already within you to make you godly. (2 Peter 1:3-4)
- Suicide destroys plans for your future. (Jeremiah 29:11)
- Suicide rejects God's commitment to work in your circumstances for good. (Romans 8:28)

– Suicide denies God's overall goal to transform you into the character of Christ (Romans 8:29)
– Suicide rejects God's right to have you offer yourself up in worship to Him. (Romans 12:1)
– Suicide rejects God's desire to have you function within the body of Christ. (Romans 12:4-5)

Practicalities

Practical Insights for Recovery

Moving beyond survival and through to stability can be very difficult. Healing to a place of success in transformed thinking and living takes coming to terms with all that has happened. It takes a lot of time, growing in grace, mercy to be kind through the process, and a vested support system. This has worked in my life, and I have coached others through similar plights to work through recovery that is rooted in Scripture. The process is not merely positive thinking. It is everything opposite of what attempting to die by suicide is between the individual and God. It is a submission of the most liberating kind, and it is a daily and sometimes a moment by moment determination that pays off in dividends of restored confidence, affirmed identity in Christ, purpose, and passion to thrive. It is the joy that God's grace is truly greater than all sin.

When a person survives an attempt, there is a complexity of stigma involved that one cannot know unless they have lived experience. General stigma comes from others and can include reactionary withdrawal or other behaviors including, but not limited to, discrimination, gossip, labeling, avoidance, and fear of reoccurrence. Trust for the person who made the attempt to die is damaged, and in many cases lost permanently. There are a litany of opinions and judgments that conclude the act was selfish, attention-seeking, or manipulative. To that end, I will encourage revisiting all seven of the suicides mentioned in the Bible (Judges 9:54, Judges 16:30, 1 Samuel 31:4, 1 Samuel 31:5, 2 Samuel 17:33, 1 Kings 16:18, and Matthew 27:5).

It is unwise to conclude that one knows what was in the mind of the offender, especially if you have never been to such a vexed state of mind, body, and soul. I can attest that in my case, as is the case with many others, the mind is in chaos, however, the body experiences physical pain as I had never known before or since. It is not all mental, and it does impact the soul.

One may conclude that suicide attempts are rooted in manipulation and perhaps selfishness to regain control of dire straits but be careful with what is spoken to attempt survivors. As believers in Christ, we must value the power of words and their ability to talk about life and death. Assuredly there is more going through the mind of the one in need of recovery than even he or she can grasp. Statements like: "You did this for attention," "You were just being manipulative," are opinions from a place of grief. Once these words fall on a wounded soul, they cannot be undone. The person who attempted suicide already knows what he or she has done. Furthermore, the enemy will wreak havoc taking such statements and doing everything possible to use those opinions to plant seeds of doubt that can rapidly progress into wrong beliefs. Erroneous beliefs can increase the risk of the individual feeling unsupported and alone in a battle to survive. They can also increase the risk of repeated attempts to stop the pain. The toughest part of the fight for me, and I have since learned the same is true from other attempt survivors, was resisting the temptation to give in to what others thought of me. Hence scripture's life-power. I quickly learned to ask aloud, "Who then am I trying to please, God or man? It was a simple question, but one that came with the awareness of my body and soul's struggle to release invisible fetters that sought to keep me down. When I regained brief consciousness while on life support, my soul knew what had happened while my mind did not know where I was. My body lay restrained as I slipped back into unconsciousness. A machine was used to sustain my life as my body was detoxed. I vaguely remember slipping off to sleep so aware that God had saved me.

An attempt survivor may be dealing with the complications and consequences of bodily injury that is either temporarily impaired, disfigured, or forever altered. Words spoken to the person to make a difference are essential because self-talk is entirely infused by enemy noise. This perspective leans heavily on spiritual insight. The psychological will not be ignored but will be left to those that practice (with an emphasis on practice) behavioral health. It has been my experience and observation that there is a considerable margin of error when the whole person's breakdown is not addressed. We are spiritual beings and thought science demands empirical data. The measure of a man is only known by God. So, the spirit and thoughts of man can be counseled best when beliefs and their foundations are processed in biblical counseling. As a man thinks, so he is, and if he is willing to be submitted to God for transformation, that truth does not get packed with the lies that I know I wrestled with. Those lies include the fear of wondering what others would say about me and the fear that I would never be thought of in any other way again. I learned to keep God's Word central as I learned how to take these thoughts captive. Sorting through lies became a habit of transformation that now can very naturally identify the lies and seize the seeds before they take root in my mental real estate. My mind, body, and soul belong to God. Stewardship of His grace to give an attempt survivor another chance to continue living according to His purpose for life is a decision of submission that came by repentance and a sorrowful heart.

For the very reason that a person survives, believers of all people should be willing to submit to so great an opportunity for God to work in and through us. Yes, it means taking steps through refining fires that we can trust will prove our faith of greater worth than pure gold. Who can put a price on the life of the one that failed to usurp God's Lordship in their life? Just as I was then, I am now; a loved, daughter of the King. That He would choose to rescue me, when I acted against His Lordship to take my life, is mercy. I am more compelled than ever to live out His call on my life.

The stigma that an attempt survivor struggles with differs from that of survivors of a loved one lost to suicide. It is vital to understand that both deal with it. The moral injury each caused and sustained by the act of attempting to kill. The complexity of shame or embarrassment is amplified in the attempt survivor by something referred to as a double stigma. Double stigma occurs within the suicide attempt survivor. He or she survived an attempt on his/her life and now has convictions and judgements about what did not go as planned. Surviving, while miraculous and a gift of grace, creates a moral dilemma. It is a crushing and vulnerable place that involves self-talk, listening for words of hope, and the enemy's accusations that come as lies disguised as truth.

THE LAZARUS PRINCIPLE

This is a prime time to remember Lazarus and the vital example to "be available." It is a time and opportunity to be ready to help take off the graveclothes. The sooner someone can see through the lens of scripture how God sees them, and the less chaos the enemy has to validate lies, the better. It starts with being present. It means you, the believer in Christ, must learn to take every thought captive and submit every opinion and judgment to Him as you avail your presence to someone that very likely hurt you.

You may feel like Martha did—that the whole situation stinks! It does. Remember that Lazarus was not left alone in his resurrected state, Jesus commanded those closest in relationship to Lazarus and believer in Christ to remove his bindings. Recovery requires community.

PRACTICAL PRINCIPLES FOR RECOVERY SUPPORT

Peer support is God's plan. (Proverbs 27:17)

A ministry of presence mitigates isolation and provides evidence that a survivor is not being treated coldly by everyone. (Ecclesiastes 4:11)

Accountability through Scripture. (Ecclesiastes 4:12)

Validation for the person and provision of a safe place of conversation without judgment. (Proverbs 1:5)

Acknowledgement of what is said. Only speak as the Lord prompts words of life. (Proverbs 16:1-3)

Seek to understand and leave the results to God. Validation of the importance of that person to you from their point of view. (Proverbs 3:5-6)

Providing hope for the future. (Proverbs 4:20)

Be part of a support team. There will be much that the person has to work out with God, through counseling or therapy. Support as a team is indispensable. (Proverbs 17:17)

Keep confidentiality.[63] Be a trust builder and allow the trust to build. (Proverbs 11:13, 20:19)

Have a plan with clearly defined roles. An excellent tool available as an app is called Elijah. It has three designated persons (for a support team) that the survivor can reach out to simultaneously. The push of one button sends a text to the team. This is not intended to be used in place of calling 911. It sends the location of the person in distress to the text recipients who can then call 911 if it is deemed necessary. A responder can get on the scene much faster than a support team. It could be the person only needs to talk through a rough moment. (Psalm 41:1)

Speak life and impart biblical counsel. (Proverbs 15:4, 15:28, 16:24, 25:11)

---

63   There must be an understanding that any legitimate concern for self-harm will be addressed according to a plan to keep the survivor safe, even from his own desire to isolate if things spoken indicate a safety threat.

POINTS OF CONSIDERATION

Initial trust can take years to develop. The incident that broke trust was like a bucket full of water, kicked over and emptied. The bucket may be upright again but imagine that the bucket now has many holes. Trust is established one drop of water in the bucket at a time. Some things will make significant deposits, others will be like a tiny mist. Rest assured that your bucket will be refilled with consistent and persistent effort over time. The situation requires two willing parties to agree either to start fresh, as if to have a new empty bucket, or to work with a worn-out bucket, repairing the holes as you go. Either is a work in submission to allow the Lord to rebuild the trust as each one works to move forward from the event. Both require honesty that trust is damaged. This needs to be understood as an opportunity to build trust, not fear. Trust is a work in progress. You cannot trust what has not proven faithful. You can both trust the Lord to accomplish what is right. He is always faithful.

UNDERSTAND EXPECTATIONS

Everyone has unspoken expectations. Be aware and honest about yours. An attempt survivor may expect compassion and grace. It does not come naturally. When hurt led to an act of attempted suicide, it transferred pain and caused grief. The person did not need to die, what needs to die is our demanding flesh suppressing our spiritual selves from allowing our hope and expectation to be solely in the Lord. Working through the pain is involved in healing. The survivor and those impacted by the attempt will be best served the sooner each releases the other from expectations. The loved one often has an expectation that the person knows why or can satisfactorily provide answers that he has no adequate response to. That is why questioning is better served by asking "How?" How will I allow this situation to let God work in me to be who He created me to be? To be sure, it was a significant tragedy, but it must be left in the past while dealing with the repercussions in the present, to have a healthier future. Refrain from bringing up what someone did as if to communicate that incident as their new identity.

REFINING FAITH

Identity and growth beyond any tragedy require that we go to the Healer for full restoration. Growth does not occur in a comfort zone. Shadrach, Meshach, and Abednego exemplified trust and how to face courageously what God may allow. Everyone wants a miracle, but most are not willing to withstand what they must for the miracle to occur.

Submission in faith is to let God be the Lord of all areas of our lives, be it health, brokenness, and need for spiritual maturity. You can trust God to bring about what is right, even when you have done wrong. You have been given faith. Embrace it. Are you available for your faith to be refined?

PART THREE:
TRIUMPH OVER TRAGEDY —
A PERSONAL TESTIMONY

CRISIS RESPONSE PROCESS

THE SPIRITUAL SIZE-UP

As an emergency responder, one of the first things taught and repeatedly emphasized is the importance of sizing up a situation. There is a rapid nine-step process that starts with gathering facts. As Christians, the value of emergency preparedness is something to consider in the context of spiritual struggles. It is not a matter of *if* we will face trials, it is a matter of *when*. Are you prepared? Do you have a strategy or a plan? My husband chuckles at my response to national weather alerts. I go on high alert. He does not. But he has not been part of destruction recovery, care, or post-trauma psychological care. Spiritual warfare is necessary for the world we live in. It is not something to be avoided in mentoring and equipping believers. To that end, the extreme of teaching that everything that goes wrong is demonic is also as dangerous as the boy crying wolf. Eventually, no one listened to him when there was an actual danger. The need for clarity to take appropriate action is why a process and plan are important.

GATHER THE FACTS

What has gone wrong?

It is essential to know and discern between everyday life happenings versus apparent spiritual attack or warfare. It is unwise to be of the mindset that every time something goes wrong or when you experience a series of challenges that you are under spiritual attack. We are fallen, sin-impacted people. Missing the mark is sin, and no matter how nicely you want to hear it, it is not loving to tiptoe around the truth that restores. You and I are not perfect, and we need help! The cause of challenges or things gone awry can be the consequence of sin. For example, a woman who was raped did not sin through her attire or behavior. Someone else's sin impacted her. To suggest she was to blame would be irresponsible and cruel. Gather the facts of what has led to your challenge. I attempted suicide. Attempting to take my own life, no matter what led to the moment, was a fact I had to face. I acted contrary to what is holy. God is the giver and sustainer of life. My days were written in the book of life before one of them came to be. Without sufficient guidance from scripture, it is somewhat easy to misalign with the enemy in thoughts and beliefs that indeed are the belief of a lie. Satan and demonic forces are not to blame for all hardships in life. As a church, too often, we tend to confront people about their pain instead of being available to minister in kindness and with compassion. When you and I are broken, grace and mercy are very much needed.

ASSESS AND COMMUNICATE THE DAMAGE

Words have the power of life and death. When spoken aloud, something happens in the spiritual realm that most people are oblivious to or do not consider. Consider this, Satan is the prince of the power of the air. God created everything, including Satan and all humanity. Stewardship is something commonly considered in the context of the use of words that are spoken aloud. The book of Proverbs contains over one-hundred and nineteen verses that detail the benefit of speaking words in wisdom. It also warns what can result in the careless use of our speech. One perfect example is Proverbs 13:3 The one who guards his mouth preserves his life; The one who opens wide his lips comes to ruin. There is a time to speak and a time to remain silent. Incredibly, the power of words spoken at just the right time, to a key person or group of people,

can change the world. King Solomon even emphasized the value of
wisdom to be more than strength. A whisper has more impact than
shouting. Moreover, such understanding is better than weapons of
war.[64] That is a vital declaration when you consider that the most
potent weapon in your spiritual arsenal is prayer.

Poor stewardship of our words—with others or with the
Lord—gives our enemy a foothold into areas of our life. Falling
prey to deception often happens unknowingly. No one wants to be
deceived. Ignorance may be bliss to some, but the ramifications of
ignorance can also get you in a bad situation. In Acts 5, Sapphira
knew that she and her husband had withheld from the collective
giving. She was given the chance to answer honestly, but she lied.
Her carelessness with words at a critical moment cost her life.

Truth is not subjective. The objective source of all truth is the
fullness of our triune God. His Word is our point of reference.
The Lord God Almighty is always the Mighty LORD, and we are
His people. The vast difference between him and us is that He
remains holy and is always the same. We are human, imperfect,
can waiver, and are the specific targets of the enemy, who desires to
keep us from fully realizing God's plan for our lives. The enemy is
a liar and is hell-bent on robbing God of His glory. We must take
responsibility for our role in what may be out of alignment with
God's desires for us. A person can misalign himself or herself into
the enemy camp on account of our human shortcomings. God
wants to transform those and bring reconciliation with Himself,
but when we do not, we are not aligned with Him. When we align
with the Lord, His work is accomplished in and through us. Just
like when we turned to Christ for salvation, we continually need to
turn away from lies to the truth. Daily we have the opportunity to
turn away from the enemy and toward God. Satan seeks to under-
mine our minds, bodies, and souls. God gives life. Transformation
is God's work, our part is "to be" transformed. In other words, we
need to agree that we need transforming of our minds and then
be available for the Lord to help us through the process. It is far

---

64 Ecclesiastes 9:16-18

more straightforward to align with God and let Him do the work of transformation than to think it is up to us. We complicate matters too much. While it is a simple way, it is not always natural or comfortable.

CONSIDER THE PROBABILITIES

What can God do when you trust Him with the truth?
Can you trust God to care for your pain?
When you feel the ripple effect of sin that others have done or kept hidden, it is common to carry guilt that is not yours to carry. It is awful when another's sin touches your life. Unfortunately, it is inevitable. There are casualties of war, and many people are part of the collateral damage. The good news that God is for you and that hope prevails!

When I was very young, a young neighborhood friend did something that hurt and violated me. It scared me, and I immediately felt awful inside, but I did not know why. I was too young to know then that what had been done to me was evil. I believe the other person did not know it was evil either. She wanted to show me a leather whip and how one of her relatives played a game with her. Initially, I was impressed and eager to see it. In my mind, only cowboys knew how to use that kind of whip. We went into a shed, where she showed me what she knew to do with that whip, and I was sexually molested.

Later in my walk with Christ, I remembered the incident, and God spoke about it to me through Scripture. Scripture teaches that behaviors can lead to generational sin. This happens when behaviors or coping skills are learned and passed onto subsequent generations. When someone grows up not knowing anything different, and becomes a byproduct of his or her environment, it is not uncommon that destructive habits form and ruinous behaviors continue. But they need not be permanent! God promises deliverance and healing. My places of brokenness and the desecration of my tiny temple was not my fault. Still, the impact left residual feelings of guilt that I should never have carried. The enemy is a liar and accuser, and people who experience trauma can easily latch onto things that are just not true. I learned the promise that God would bless the one that turned to Him to a thousand generations. This meant that I had hope! Although I was not great at math, I knew a thousand was a more significant number than three and four. I marvel at the fact that each time a person chooses to let God accomplish His work in you, that choices sets in motion blessings that start with that generation and continue into others. When those around you are impacted by your witness, they become part of the thousand. It is a tremendous promise to cling to.

ASSESS YOUR OWN SITUATION

You and I must learn to take our responsibility to cling to God's promises and leave responsibility with the truly guilty individual. I was not responsible for what was done to me. I was an innocent child until it happened. I do not blame the neighbor, for she had learned something from an adult. That adult was the person responsible—my friend was as much of a victim as I was. Not knowing better, I was molested by two other children before I reached first grade, and later abused in my youth. That one act led to my keeping silent in future hurts. I was not taught that things like that were wrong. It only felt wrong, and I felt worse every time it happened. As I grew, I became aware of a need to forgive in order to let God heal the brokenness. This awareness developed over time. The positive outcome was that God healed my brokenness, and I equipped my children early in life to know what was appropriate and was inappropriate, according to God's desire for them. Pain can be destructive, but it can also become constructive and productive in God's hands.

ESTABLISH PRIORITIES

We must only take responsibility for what we have control over, be it our actions or our thoughts. Sin is any thought, action, or words spoken that go against God's holiness and what He declares as honoring behavior. There are times we miss the mark in ignorance and the Father enables us to receive forgiveness by His grace.[65] We do have the responsibility of learning and doing things differently to the glory of God as we mature spiritually.

My highest priority as an eager maturing Christian is to serve God to the best of my ability and not to become puffed up with knowledge. I desire to know Him so intimately that I pass along how amazing His love is. It is my conviction and God-given privilege to pass along what He has revealed. I have learned this only by the guidance of His Word and Holy Spirit.

MAKE DECISIONS

What can you do that will glorify God?

I caution you not to credit Satan with what is not due to him. He relishes when we believe the lies and exalt him rather than humbling ourselves and asking the Lord to reveal truth through reflection. God receives more glory when you and I start to gain a deeper understanding of who is truly at work in and through you. God! The progression of growth laid out in 2 Peter 1:5-8 is both a list of goals and an evaluation checklist that I use for self-evaluation. When applied, God's perfect love casts out fear and establishes God's authority in your thought process. Then you can exercise diligence, experience increased faith, and gain moral excellence. Knowledge increases and your spiritual being will desire self-control. Perseverance will be a byproduct of the progress. Increased brotherly kindness will be the muscle memory of matured new habits. Diligence in these actions of virtue will produce the fruit of the spirit. I caution you to focus on self-evaluation, as to whether your behavior is honoring or dishonoring to God in words, thoughts, or actions. Is what you are listening to or looking at consistent with growth in an honest relationship between you and God?

---

65 Acts 17:30

For if these qualities are yours and are increasing, they render you neither useless nor unfruitful in the true knowledge of our Lord Jesus Christ. For he who lacks these qualities is blind or short-sighted, having forgotten his purification from his former sins.
— 2 Peter 1:8-9

TAKE ACTION

What must you do differently? Do you have a clear emergency plan?

To perform well in emergency response situations, drills are conducted in times of preparation, so that muscle memory is built. That, in turn, translates to performance that is an intentional response and not an emotional fight-or-flight reaction. God forbid that you freeze in the crosshairs of your enemy's high-powered arsenal of lies that will lead to doubt in who you are in Christ.

With full disclosure, reflecting on what God brought me through and insight did not come to fullness until long after I healed from the trauma of acting to take my own life. I had made a marriage vow. I meant that vow, and did all I could to accomplish it. I will not forget what a blow it was to realize that by swearing to God something that I could not do, I opened myself up to spiritual vulnerability. My best intentions did not matter. I had spoken it out loud and meant with all that was in me that I would make something happen. I had no idea what I had done. When I did sense in my spirit that something was wrong, I had no idea what it was. I believed my vow to be an extraordinary commitment that I intended to keep.

I heard it said not to make a rash vow, but I did not know what that meant . The word vow had one context to me—couples exchange vows at a wedding. I had not considered or learned that a vow is a promise, pledge, or swearing of an oath to someone about something. I had no idea that I was incapable of keeping a promise I genuinely wanted to keep. Furthermore, I was oblivious to what could result from breaking it. Had I known I would not have promised God that I would do whatever it took to make a marriage work; even if it cost me my life. I had grown up a child of divorce and was adamant not to allow that kind of devastation to touch my future children. This set me up to believe a lie.

I actually thought when I made that vow that I could keep it. Unfortunately, marriage cannot be about one person working hard; it is about both committed to working at it no matter what happens. I could only uphold *my* commitment. The vow itself was impossible. A marriage takes three, willing, active, and participating parties working toward the same goal of unity and peace. Hopefully, the couple also seeks to honor God. God could and would uphold His part. You and I cannot make another person do what he or she is not willing to do for himself. No matter how much we want something for him. We are imperfect people. The vow exchange in marriage must be a commitment to let God be God at all times. The lie that I believed was naive at best, spiritually ignorant for sure, and an important lesson learned. I learned the importance of mentorship and how to prevent forfeiture of sacred space in my mind.

EVALUATE PROGRESS

Every believer's journey is different, and we grow at difference paces. As we invest in our relationship with the Lord, He meets us and guides us into all truth. Getting to know my Lord and triune God has been a journey that reminds me continually—and you must know, too—that He is not finished with you. You can trust Him. He does not waste any hurt. He redeems even what the world thinks is irreconcilable.

Your progress will vary from time to time. We live in a world that wants expedient results. People tend to not be patient to wait. We demand what we want, right now. However, God's timing is not on-demand. The appearance of silence form God does not mean He is absent, nor is His stillness a lack of His working. Wise counsel is important. Draw on scripture to evaluate progress and remember that vision, blueprint, and preparation are God's plan. Do not ask if something is a spiritual attack. For a believer, the times of absolute warfare or perceived attack in which advanced emergency planning is needed will kick in. When all hell breaks loose, you will maintain stability.

START OVER AGAIN

Situations will arise and be resolved. The next time a situation arises, you will be at a different place in your spiritual journey. This is how children of God move through life's difficulties. Paul reminds us to press toward the mark that you are called to in Christ Jesus. His strategy was to forget what was behind him. That he had persecuted the early church had no more significance to his present and future than Peter's denial of Christ had to Peter's future .

Know this, Beloved, there will be spiritual battles, but Christ won the war. Past events may be brought up and be sure you know that the enemy will accuse, lie, and try to cheat you out of your God-given identity. What matters most now, and especially in moments of crisis, is who Christ says you are. Like the apostles Paul, Peter, and many other saints who have gone before you, your identity is secure as is your future. Jesus is the only author and perfecter of your faith.

SUMMARY PRINCIPLES AND ACTIVATION OF A SPIRITUAL SIZE UP

Gather facts. What happened, how many people appear to be involved? What is my current situation? (Proverbs 15:22) Activating fact-gathering is important, and in doing so, be objective and include a mentor or spiritually discerning person who will keep confidentiality as you share what happened. If it is difficult to stick to facts personally, ask for that specific feedback from the listener's perspective. There are times we are too close to the situation emotionally to see something other than our view.

Assess and communicate the damage. Are you in danger of spiritual vulnerability that alters the ability to see yourself as God sees you and the situation? Are you at risk of believing a lie? You must activate honesty as you confess your vulnerability, hurts, fears, thoughts about others, and feelings towards others. God already knows what's gone on. Unleash to your spiritual arsenal of truth on the enemy. Let the Holy Spirit be your helper. If you are not sure what to pray, allow the Holy Spirit to lead you. (Mark 4:23)

Consider the probabilities. What could happen if nothing is done? What could God do with your trust and increased faith? (Exodus 20:5-6) Consider what role sin has in the current situation. God is approachable, He knows the struggle, and He has made a way forward from the tragedy.

Assess your situation. Is there a need to turn away from sin personally? If it is someone else's sin, let yourself off the hook. (1 Corinthians 10:13) God has made a way to resist every temptation, even to hold onto guilt that may not be your own to take. Guilt is the result of a planned and executed act. Do not carry guilt from tragic outcomes that came about because of the sin of someone else or because of tragic happenings. The way out of that messy lie the enemy would want you to believe is to know that the truth will set you free. (John 8:32)

Establish priorities. Who will you serve in this moment concerning this situation? (Jeremiah 29:13) A crisis can heighten stress and muddy up your ability to think clearly. Go back to your plan and remember the objective is to glorify God. If it takes asking an accountability partner or a small group to be a support team to navigate the rough spots, surround yourself with wise counsel. (Proverbs 11:14)

Make decisions. Focus on embracing the empowerment and authority God has given you to change things according to His plan for you. Acknowledge the person you are in this instant. Be in the moment so that you can change the impact of the previous situation. Be available in giving God first place to transform your mind. The renewal available comes as you avail yourself to be processed by God's grace through His mercy. The renewal of your mind comes about miraculously because transforming the mind created by God is His work. Decisions are powerful! (Joshua 24:15)

Develop a plan. Develop a plan to help you accomplish your priorities. Simple ideas can be verbal, more detailed plans can be written down. Activation will bring about what has been planned and prepared for, similar to how fire drills prepare for an actual fire. Have a plan before it is ever needed. Draw from the wisdom of others. (Psalm 127:1, Proverbs 16:3)

Take action. Execute your plan, document deviations, and spiritual status changes so that you can go before the Lord honestly, humbly, and for counsel from Him. (Proverbs 4:25, Ecclesiastes 8:5-7, and Luke 9:62)

Evaluate progress. At intervals, evaluate your progress in accomplishing objectives, and determine what needs adjustment, growth, or development to stabilize and strengthen you or improve your situation. (Proverbs 1:5, 14:15)

PERSONAL TESTIMONY — MY CRISIS

MIND AND MINE FIELDS

Your mind is your greatest asset as well as your most significant liability. It can be transformed through renewal by the Lord, and in it, we can hold great debates of self-talk. At times, your self-talk quite convincingly may present as lies, accusations, and identity theft. Within your own mind, your thoughts can be the argumentative voices of others that can develop into deeply rooted beliefs. They can seize your confidence and self-image. They can prevent courage from breaking through so you can achieve greatness. The mind is a battlefield. Though the good news is that the war has already been won, we all still have battles. Battles can kick our tales, build our strength, or break us. A person's brokenness is not an end unto itself. It can be a new beginning. For a Christian, hope is the Father, Son and Savior, and His Holy Spirit in us. If you know your life is continually in the process of being made more like Christ and purged of the perishable things that are corrupt, you can take hold of Scripture and know that there is no blunder so great that it will mess up God's perfect plan.

From the apostle Paul[66] to us today, this means that any struggle we may succumb to—including addiction, depression, grief, anxiety, or any other mental crisis that leads to shocking behavior—you can know that God has already made provision for good through the promise secured for every believer in Christ's death, burial, and resurrection. That does not mean we go out and run amuck doing, saying, or ingesting whatever we want. A Christ-follower is, after all, the temple of the living God. That is a literal fact. The Holy Spirit with which we are sealed abides in us. He is Our helper, God's ever-present help, counselor, power, and teacher. Your mind is neither brain nor thoughts alone. Amazingly, your mind is comprised of ideas, thoughts, opinions, beliefs, and it forms convictions and judgments, all while storing information into the brain. All that circuitry miraculously contributes to every system's function of your body. The Bible has much to say about our mind, heart, and soul, but only one is physical and tangible—the heart. The mind is much more than your brain or and more complex than cerebral neuroscience. Modern technology can reveal activity correlating with certain things we do and say. There are limitations even to science, especially in measuring the thoughts of man. Science can identify the impact of thinking, but it cannot know a thought. Only God can do that.

When we embrace the truths of Scripture and subject ourselves to things we cannot explain, we can then cast our gaze toward the Lord. We can worship and marvel at the miraculous, for we know the source is our Almighty God. The awe of being created in His image factors into your understanding and what you embrace in faith. For as he thinks within himself, so he is.[67]

Only God knows the mind of man, and it is fascinating how Scripture discusses the subject.

> *The heart is more deceitful than all else And is desperately sick; Who can understand it? I, the Lord, search the heart, I test the mind, Even to give to each man according to his ways, According to the results of his deeds.*[68]

The Hebrew word לֵב translated as heart literally means by extension, the inner person, self, the seat of thought and emotion, conscience, courage, mind, and understanding. God tests

---

67   Proverbs 23:7
68   Jeremiah 17:9-10

the mind; אכפת [69] also means kidney; inmost being; heart, mind, spirit, the seat of thought; the emotion of the inner person "the reins."[70] The profound depth of this is revelatory when we consider that the purpose of the urinary system is to filter out toxins from the bloodstream. Some fluid or toxins get reabsorbed by the body, but most get expelled as urine. We are so wonderfully made, God knew that even our toxicity could not be overlooked or dismissed. He designed the human body to sustain wellness. The Lord knows to what end the impact such toxicity has on each individual. This should cause us to quake in awe of how intricate life balance is when it comes to overall health. The imbalance of our God-designed systems impacts our total health and more pointedly can impact other system's functions in the human body, including mental health. People that need dialysis to live know well the importance of purging toxic waste from the body and how neglect can compromise overall health. The mind works the same way.

A deep dive into scripture's use of the word *mind* and how often it links to *kidneys* led to asking myself: How often have I really taken into account what idle or wicked thoughts may impact more than my mind? A landmark experiment back in the 1980s, conducted by psychologist Eric Klinger of the University of Minnesota,

---

69 The purpose of the urinary system is to filter out excess fluid and other substances from your bloodstream. Simply Put, our kidneys detox the blood which is essential to a well-performing body. http://sciencenetlinks.com/student-teacher-sheets/organ-systems/ Organ Systems; Urinary System.

70 Interlinear Bible Jeremiah 17:10 *"I, Jehovah, search the heart; I try the reins even to give to each man according to his ways, according to the fruit of his doings."* and Strongs H3820 "a from of H3824; the heart, als used (figuartively) very widely for the feelings, the will, and even intellect; likewise the center of anything; -care for, comfortably, consent, considered, courageous, friendly…" H3824 "the heart (as the interior most organ)." See also Revelation 2:23 *"I will strike her children dead. Then all the churches will know that I am he who searches hearts and minds, and I will repay each of you according to your deeds."* and Strongs G3520 *nephros* "of uncertain affinity; a kidney (plural), i.e. (figuratively) the inmost mind:--reins."

tracked volunteers to record what they were thinking whenever a handheld device chirped over a week. What was discovered was that within a 16-hour day, people may have about five hundred thoughts that are unintentional and "intrusive." Such thoughts lasted about fourteen seconds on average. While most dealt with the concerns of everyday life, eighteen percent were unacceptable, uncomfortable, or just plain bad—politically incorrect or mean thoughts. Thirteen percent of thoughts were ugly, out of character, or downright shocking—say murderous or perverse ideas. To the tune of one-hundred-sixteen minutes a day, the mind is intruded upon by unwanted, unwelcome, or unhelpful thoughts that steal joy, deplete stamina, and alter us in ways seldom considered.[71] Consider that the study was conducted in the 1980s when there were no handheld electronics that could access the internet with the tip of a finger. There is a greater need today to be very mindful of what feeds our mind and body. What our minds feasts or snacks upon continually is critical. If it is not righteous, we can succumb easily to temptation in our thoughts, which will impact our entire being inclusive of strength physically, emotionally, and spiritually. This begs the question of personal introspect: How then precisely and individually do we love the Lord with all our heart, mind, and strength? That is a meditative and contemplative question we would do well to ask our heavenly Father. We must ask Him to help us be transformed by the renewal of the mind. We must learn what it is and how thoughts are taken captive to the glory of God.

When we realize that chaotic situations can result in the entire body reacting in survival mode, we can be assured that God knows what is taking place in the moment, even when we have no clue. A completely natural reaction of flight, fight, or freeze can result in behavior that, in hindsight, comes into question following a triggered survival mode of operation. Depending on the person thoughts can deteriorate rapidly. An excellent example of this is seen through Elijah the prophet following his victory over

---

71   Jena E Pincott, *Wicked Thoughts*. Psychology Today. September 1, 2015
     in *I Declare War*. by Levi Lusko, p. 43.

the prophets of Baal. His retreat into a cave and what he said are indicative of what can happen after a great God-victory through His people. We can be caught off-guard and out of character.[72]

We must come to value the importance of learning skills to sustain a sound mind and we must be aware how our mortal enemy uses chaos, depression, grief, and many other emotions to till the soil of a spiritual battlefield. When we fail to realize that mental stewardship is crucial, we remain ignorant of the advantage we give the enemy. He will strategically work to lure the weary or heavy-burdened soul. This is something I wish that I'd had a mentor to help me learn more about in my Christian journey. We must learn how to guard the mind and be aware when any one of us is in a vulnerable spot. Scripture mandates we guard our hearts and minds. It is to be done in Christ Jesus; in His body with the support of other believers capable of supporting us in battle. Just like Aaron and Hur supported Moses as Joshua battled Amalek. No one should ever fight alone.[73]

After my crisis, the Holy Spirit led me through a spiritual boot camp. It was an intensely reflective, meditative time during which I received much spiritual insight. It was as if what I went through left me with spiritual visibility that is hard to explain. I do know the source is the Holy Spirit, and how He has equipped me helps me to be well aware of things I cannot touch but can see. I now recognize how emotions are given to bless us. Knowing what is transpiring in thought, body, and soul, or how to realize that emotions are the sensation and byproduct of what the human eye cannot see, is a gift.

Often we do not realize how our body communicates nonverbally. Our bodies can communicate to us through soreness, illness, or sadness. Now I have a more profound passion for helping others know how to take up the armor of God, and I more fully appreciate the freedom for which Christ died to set the captives free. Lord knows I fell captive to much in ignorance, and I am thankful God

72   1 Kings 19:4
73   Exodus 17:10-12

overlooks sin committed in ignorance. "Being then the children of God, we ought not to think that the Divine Nature is like gold or silver or stone, an image formed by the art and thought of man. Therefore having overlooked the times of ignorance, God is now declaring to men that all people everywhere should repent, because He has fixed a day in which He will judge the world in righteousness through a Man whom He has appointed, having furnished proof to all men by raising Him from the dead."[74] With the assurance of a risen Savior, we can be assured that we, in our identity in Christ, are also resurrected when we repent following any blunder.

The enemy is a liar! We must not step into a snare of pride or arrogance to ever believe that we can never succumb to deception. We must know the Holy Spirit, commune intimately with our Savior, and we must know His Word so that when the inauthentic subtleties come against wounded souls in vulnerable times of desperation, we will stand firm against the devil's schemes. God's unchanging truth prevails even in the darkest moments.

Some of what I learned coming out of the pit blew me away. In increasing measure, truths of Scripture would prompt thoughts that were contrary to honoring God while I was in the midst of my depression. For months I cried out, feeling as though my life was like an unraveling rope in a fierce round of tug-o-war. It still irritates me to realize how crafty the enemy is. It was not like I did not know Scripture and my Lord. It was not that I did not trust Christ. I did. I trusted Him implicitly. That season of grief deluged every moment in immense chaotic pain. It was so bad that even Scripture and its truths were used to manipulate me. It is true that Satan will disguise himself as an angel of light. His servants also disguise themselves as servants of righteousness. It is a life-or-death matter that we remain intimate with our knowledge of the Father. I could not appreciate this more than the instant the presence of God's Spirit broke through my chaos. He found me in the blinding darkness of the abyss I was in when all hell had broken loose to take me out of my right mind and out of this world. It happened

74 Acts 17:29-31

one subtle step at a time. My breaking point was the end of a twenty-year marriage that I did not want to end. God honestly knew there were things about it that I did want to stop. Things that did not honor Him, things that broke His heart. The mercies of God are new every day, and with free will we choose every decision we make. The sovereignty of God will allow us to go astray as He patiently waits for our return for restoration.

The lies believed in a weary season can come as subtleties from the enemy. They tend to impact or compromise health and wellness cumulatively. Sometimes the outcomes include illness or varied forms of a health crisis. I knew I was tired. I was weary physically, academically, and emotionally.

I had come to suffer from chronic migraines and struggled with depression, which in hindsight, I realize was more situational and post-traumatic stress related than chronic depression. I had no idea then that the sleep disorder I was tested for was to identify stress-related or more serious causes of illness as I earnestly strived to continue in a call to minister and to be further equipped to serve others. I did not know then about PTSD, about which I have since learned. It seemed I could grasp that my mind was on overload, still, I strived to keep enough balance to manage a situation out of my control. I took a sabbatical from a full scholarship PhD, and that was almost as painful as losing the marriage. I felt that I was a poor steward. Yet, I knew that being available for my kids was a priority. I lost my job due to a no-divorce policy. I lost my marriage and believed that I would lose in-laws as a family and would be in an endless battle with family. My experience of divorce as a child gripped me with fear as every indication already appeared that I would be the one ousted and sided against during this divorce. Throughout my childhood, I had been a child of four divorces.

The heart does not know biological ties. When it chooses to love, it loves. When people are ripped out of one's life, soul wounds occur as the mind is scarred and entangled by emotions that can wreak havoc with all manner of toxic thoughts that accompany a broken heart: rejection, abandonment, low self-esteem, insecurity.

The list of probable outcomes is unique to each situation. Scripture is very clear about hope deferred leading to a sick heart. Thankfully I can look back and receive the new mercies of each day, as I continue to thrive in life. It is the mercy and grace of Adonai, God Most High, that He would be with me through every moment of my breaking and through the brokenness to allow me to live.

My grieved, soul-sick, vulnerable, and weary self was in a catastrophic storm. The conditions, no doubt, caused the licking of chops for the hungry lion and thief that had come to steal and kill and destroy my life. Indeed, the enemy sought and found who he may devour. I was so exhausted mentally that I could not see how my adversary, the devil, was prowling around like a roaring lion, seeking to devour me! As in nature, the most vulnerable become the menu. I love how powerful a counselor and very present help in times of trouble the Holy Spirit is. The very verse whispered in the chaos was also the saving grace of breakthrough when my Counselor penetrated every fiber of my being with a resounding question. A subtle whisper of the enemy taunted me with this: "Doesn't the Bible say if you are weary and heavy-laden, God will give you rest?" *Yes, I knew it did.* "Doesn't it say God will give you rest?"

Here is where the Holy Spirit broke through for me. Rest is the Hebrew word *Shalom.* In its entire meaning it is rest, peace (or absence or chaos), and to be made whole. While I could say yes to both, the taunting was to take my own life, and I acted upon doing so toxically. Even in that state I was conflicted and had so much remorse knowing what I had done. It clashed with what I thought to do, which was a complete inconsistency with every conviction I have ever held about the sanctity of life.

In all that chaos, I sensed the Holy Spirit ask, "But don't you know?" *Don't I know what?* "Do you not know that you are a temple of God and that the Spirit of God dwells in you?" With a resounding yes, I begged for my life. I confessed everything I believed about God's ability to rescue me. I knew in a way more profound than words can say that God's mercy was greater than my sin. I was fading. I was confident, and I prayed for Shalom. I was shattered to pieces, and the chaos had stopped. I felt like I could rest. Although I did not know how He would, I knew God could make me whole in Christ. Three days later, I briefly woke up on life support. That is where the journey of trauma-informed growth took hold of me on every level.

My pursuit was to press into the pure, lovely, and true. To say that I experienced shame, guilt, and shock is a grotesque under-statement. One of the precious mercies revealed was that since then, I remembered that many years ago, I had prayed for the survivor of a suicide attempt. I had such a broken heart and compassion that I asked the Lord that if He ever wanted to use me to offer hope to someone that I could not fathom what may have led to a moment of such desperate actions, I was more than willing, available, and wanted to be used for that.

I did not know how or if that prayer would be answered. It was. I am alive and so eager to live out my calling and to encourage others to keep pursuing intimacy in relationship with the Lord. The restoration He brings comes from a love that never fails. The perspective of hope, now post-trauma of a suicide attempt, I have not ever known to be addressed in the church to the boldness I have been called to minister and equip others to implement. We must fix our eyes on Christ and allow the Holy Spirit to do what only He can: teach, counsel, and help. Hope prevails. While hope deferred makes a heart sick, a longing fulfilled will surely come to pass, it is a tree of life. The confidence and assurance a child of God has is that regardless of what limitations in ignorance man has or opinions concerning suicide, Scripture condemns only blasphem-ing the Holy Spirit and God's grace is more excellent than even this sin. This is not to condone such actions as to take our lives into our own hands. Birth, life, and death are best left in the hands of our Creator. It takes more than a handful of biblical principles that includes humility, vulnerability, courage, determination, endur-ance, and perseverance to allow transformation by the renewal of the mind. You must learn to take thoughts captive and know how to silence the enemy. Believe me when I say that once a person has been in such a dark place of despair the enemy will repeatedly seek and through various agents try to keep captive a person in recovery by accusing him or her and replaying the past. Beloved, we must fix our eyes on being present. We must live to press on toward the mark for which we are called heavenward in Christ and be equipped to learn to thrive and fulfill the plan to prosper us.

Remember: God is your refuge. He can do immeasurably more than you ask or imagine. You have an enemy set on taking out of commission as many of God's soldiers called to wage war as possible. He will stop at nothing to render one dead to the mission. Whatever one may be going through may not feel good, it may be excruciating, but it is nonetheless one of the mysteries of how He is God, and we can trust Him with every hurt. It will pass. The enemy would like us to believe we must stop our pain. The truth is that suicide transfers pain from one to many. The enemy uses such grief and despair to feed lies to others who are in pain and unsupported to get through life's devastations. We must grow to serve one another more compassionately and in courage.

Now, these words that Paul wrote to the Corinthians mean more concerning the will of God than they ever could have had I not been rescued from the pit:

> *I now rejoice, not that you were made sorrowful, but that you were made sorrowful to the point of repentance; for you were made sorrowful according to the will of God, so that you might not suffer loss in anything through us. For the sorrow that is according to the will of God produces a repentance without regret, leading to salvation, but the sorrow of the world produces death. For behold what earnestness this very thing, this godly sorrow, has produced in you: what vindication of yourselves, what indignation, what fear, what longing, what zeal, what avenging of wrong! In everything, you demonstrated yourselves to be innocent in the matter. So although I wrote to you, it was not for the sake of the offender*

> *nor for the sake of the one offended, but that your earnestness on*
> *our behalf might be made known to you in the sight of God.*[75]

For this reason, we have been comforted. While I am guilty of acting to take my life, I am also not condemned for the blood of Christ cleanses me of all unrighteousness. Moreover, He has purchased my freedom from lies believed, and I am free from the pit of hell!

Depression manifests in many forms: chemical imbalance, situational, or chronic. Acts of desperation may include any or a cumulative combination of those mentioned above. Either way, distress and anguish can lead one to places one does not think he or she is capable of going. We all like to believe we have control when often there is more out of our control than we realize. A cumulative impact or series of decisions that affect individual life balance can affect reactions or elicit a response.

In my season of despair, medication was both a friend and foe. I learned far too late that had I made a correlation with how suicidal I had become in the grief, because I was often isolated by choice and left alone with few people available that I felt safe to talk to. I might have realized sooner that I was experiencing side effects. Those side effects contributed to uncharacteristic behavior. So much betrayal resulted in my pulling away from what could have been more supportive had I given people the chance to minister to me. I felt unable to speak to someone about what had become fear in my depression. I trusted no one with my wounds and trusted even less when I had thought of no longer having the will to live in pain.

We must learn to take thoughts captive. We must mentor others by modeling the practice and through prayer life. We must realize that we have a responsibility to be transformed by the renewing of the mind, but we cannot transform someone else's mind, that is God's work. We need only be available and in agreement that He is trustworthy to do it. Spiritual prescription is what we

75 2 Corinthians 7:9-12

need in the chaos of faulty thinking. Situations change when we press into our refuge and realize we cannot change ourselves. There is one we can depend on. To see the power of this directive and its outcome transformed my life.

> *Finally, brethren, whatever is true, whatever is honorable, whatever is right, whatever is pure, whatever is lovely, whatever is of good repute, if there is any excellence and if anything worthy of praise, dwell on these things.*[76]

What I regret is having no idea how fear was a factor in my depression, and spiritually it is contrary to what a child of God has every single moment of our born-again lives. To have the Holy Spirit and all He is in the life of a believer is to have a guaranteed promise.

> *The Lord has sworn And will not change His mind, "You are a priest forever"' So much the more also Jesus has become the guarantee of a better covenant.*[77]

In my deterioration of thinking, I did not know then what I do now. The Lord has given me a litmus test to use when fear creeps in, and that is to remember and ask myself if it is reverent fear for the Lord or it is scary fear that cannot be masked. And is it consistent with what God's word says that I have: "For God has not given us a spirit of timidity, but of power and love and discipline."[78] I have power over the enemy in Jesus' name. I have perfected love at my disposal. Scripture is clear on what that love is. "There is no fear in love; but perfect love casts out fear, because fear involves punishment, and the one who fears is not perfected in love."[79] Spiritual battles require that we look to the truth to dispel lies.

A believer has the discipline of a sound mind available. While a battle may torment us with thoughts and grip us in emotions, what we believe and in whom we believe can conquer chaos. Your

---

76 Philippians 4:8
77 Hebrews 7:21-22
78 2 Timothy 1:7
79 1 John 4:18

mind, body, and soul are spiritual ground. We must remember that
our body is a temple of the Lord; His Spirit abides in us. Satan has
no dominion lest we forfeit holy ground that becomes corrupt by
falling into the snare of the lie and accuser.

> *Now the salvation, and the power, and the kingdom of our
> God and the authority of His Christ have come, for the accuser of
> our brethren has been thrown down, he who accuses them before
> our God day and night. And they overcame him because of the
> blood of the Lamb and because of the word of their testimony, and
> they did not love their life even when faced with death. For this
> reason, rejoice, O heavens, and you who dwell in them. Woe to the
> earth and the sea, because the devil has come down to you, having
> great wrath, knowing that he has only a short time.*[80]

I became emotionally weighed down by every shattered piece
of my life. I seemed to have picked them all back up were carrying
them as if it were my place to do so. The subtle lie of "If it is to
be, it is up to me" proved detrimental to my healing. Eventually,
I buckled under the weight of stress and chaos of doing what only
my Lord could do for me. Only He knew what the future held, and
I was heartsick. In short, I found myself right where scripture says
is possible: "Hope deferred makes the heart sick."[81] We are never
as alone as it may feel. Friend, we need one another as support,
encouragement, and prayer warriors. Mostly we need the Shepherd
that can rescue His sheep. The Psalmist clearly understood tragedy
and despair when he wrote,

> *Why are you in despair, O my soul? And why have you be-
> come disturbed within me? Hope in God, for I shall yet praise
> Him, The help of my countenance and my God.*[82]

That passage reads like many conversations I had with the
Lord. I knew where my hope was, I did not lose hope as many

---

80   Revelation 12:10-12
81   Proverbs 13:12
82   Psalm 42:11

might assume. The hope I had was twisted and misleading to turn my focus on alleviating my pain and to prove the trust I professed. It was a sick lie. When I regained consciousness, two things were evident to me; I was angry, and I felt extreme resolve! My anger was more like fury in realizing that I had believed clever lies. I was resolved and at peace that God had saved me for a reason, and that somehow, He would use the tragedy once I was restored. I was also resolved that whatever it took, I would grow to be who God created and called me to be. To wake up with a breathing tube down my throat was mercy. For some reason, what was so chaotic to lead to my attempted suicide is so clear now. I had been detoxed and laid restrained to a bed as if I were a monster. That image is so fitting when I reflect that the enemy did his best to take captive what Christ had made free. Now I live in total freedom. Free of shame, healed of guilt, restored in mercy.

I went on to treatment and worked through so much of what I had been deceived into believing. I checked myself back in for extended care after being released and finding the shame, embarrassment was also a fertile ground of vulnerability that I was not willing to give up without a fight. That was the best thing I could have done for myself. I had no concern what stigma or shame the enemy was trying to shackle me with. I was determined to receive every bit of healing and personal growth that the Lord could bring out of me. At that treatment center, I reflected on much of what had transpired. How it happened, what I had believed, how God could use it one day. I did not ever ask the Lord why. I believed that I already had an answer from scripture that told me not to lean on my understanding. Had I been able to understand, I would likely not have found myself in the battle that I survived. I knew why; I have an enemy that will do whatever possible to keep me from fulfilling my purpose. I did often ask how: How would He have me progress? How am I to complete the call on my life? How would it change in light of what I had done? How did He want to use me? I don't have all the answers, but I did discover first-hand.

My thoughts went from thinking no one was available to believing it by the subtle fact that there was no one around. Why would there be? I did not ask for fellowship. How would anyone know when I was not honest and was very guarded about my inner turmoil? I came to believe I was alone in the battle, and by all appearances I was. The truth was that the battle was fierce, and I was suffering. Still, moments of peace sustained me physically, and clarity did ebb and flow between despairing thoughts that slid into the slippery slope of emotions. What I appreciate now about feelings is knowing we have them for God's glory. We must keep in mind that emotions are capable of driving one to poor choices. There is a reason Scripture instructs us to "Be of sober spirit, be on the alert. Your adversary, the devil, prowls around like a roaring lion, seeking someone to devour." A mind clouded by emotions is not clear. It is not thoughts alone that are unclear. The tiniest part of our brain, the pituitary, releases many enzymes and hormones that alter mind and body function. To be sober in spirit is to be clear and with the Spirit of God in control.[83] Anything less can lead to reactive behavior, acting on the whim of emotions succumbed to the vulnerability of human nature.

Emotions can work to help us. Anger itself is not bad. It is intense, and what I consider to be an essential emotion to respect for what it is. Anger is an emotion that can lead our body to scream as a cry for change reactively. Fear, if reverent awe for God, is one thing, while fearing something is a significant indicator that something is wrong and needs to change. Fear should cause us to ask if the Holy Spirit is in control? Or are we gripped by fear that can and will mislead to unsafe places, be they physical, emotional, or mental. We are instructed to put on all of it to stand against the devil's schemes. The book of Proverbs gives us a good insight into God's capability and human vulnerability.

If you are slack in the day of distress, Your strength is limited.

---

83 1 Peter 1:13 "Therefore, prepare your minds for action, keep sober in spirit, fix your hope completely on the grace to be brought to you at the revelation of Jesus Christ."

Deliver those who are being taken away to death,
And those who are staggering to slaughter, Oh hold them back.
If you say, 'See, we did not know this,'
Does He not consider it who weighs the hearts?
And does He not know it who keeps your soul?
And will He not render to man according to his work?"
— Proverbs 21:10-12

"The wise in heart will be called understanding, and sweetness of speech increases persuasiveness."[84] Hindsight is always better, and appreciating the importance of mental input is critical. No one is in the battle alone.

I desire to be a person who listens in such a way that others will be willing to talk. One of God's greatest grace gifts is greater compassion to meet others in places of pain and be used to penetrate hearts with hope and help as the Lord sees fit.

FEAR AND FAILURE TRANSFORMED

Ten years after overwhelming failures through a series of devastations, I am alive! The entire fourth chapter in Ephesians deals with Christians living in unity and maturity.

Situations that go against God's design and plan to prosper us have grievous risks and potentially devastating outcomes. Sometimes the collateral damage of choices made shatters lives in unexpected ways. I was in a horrendous spiral and alone in a fight to keep as much of my family intact as possible. Divorce is a no-win situation. The worst part was when I did ask for help, I was often told how strong I was, and that I would get through it just like I had gotten over other tragic life events. Somehow in the eyes of others I seemed to be a strong person. What no one could see were wounds carried from a multitude of traumatic events prior to the present tsunami about to plummet me to depths of grief and despair like I had never experienced or been prepared for. Others thought that all I needed was prayer. Wrong! I needed support and

84 Proverbs 16:21

evidence that I was not in that fight alone. The spiritual battle was fierce. Without evident support, the lies of the enemy were repeatedly validated by the absence of anyone present other than my kids as we went through this life-shattering nightmare.

Since experiencing such intense spiritual warfare, I have learned how to draw from my Helper, the Holy Spirit, and silence the enemy. The lies that led me into utter chaos are no more. Previously, I discussed the power of words and how to develop the discipline of using your God-given authority. Were it not for God's grace and mercy, I would not be alive nor would you be reading these truths that may help you in the spiritual battlefield. It was a sobering, life-altering moment of decision. We all have them, and what we do with our choices have repercussions—some good and some bad.

My outcome was a good one. Though my story has a good ending and ultimately glorifies God, I had some very dark days, and it has taken a lot of work and intentional growth to keep fighting the good fight. It was God's work in me and my choice to meet Him daily to be transformed which is the choice I encourage you to make every day. God is always present; you must show up for yourself every day. Traumatic transformation has led to the spiritual fruit of many ongoing transformative decisions to give my brokenness to my Heavenly Father and let Him fix all that I can identify as broken. Other traumatic transformations you may be familiar with include Saul's transformation to Paul, and Peter's reinstatement after denying Christ the night of Christ's arrest.

I know Almighty God more intimately and process His word through His Spirit in me. This helps me see things through the lens of Scripture. This lens allows me to realize that nothing I did revokes His gifts poured into me and reminds me that He asks me to do the work of an evangelist that will minister to others[85] until my last exhale. What Satan meant for evil, God continues to work for good.[86] None of this means we have free reign to do whatever

85 Romans 11:29 for the gifts and the calling of God are irrevocable.
86 Romans 8:28

we want in the name of grace. God knows your vulnerabilities, ignorance,[87] and what lies impact you, still His mercies are new, and His grace is sufficient to forgive. Friend, when you realize that you did wrong just as I did, you have an opportunity to respond in a way that radically transforms your life.[88]

It was a big day. I had auditioned and practiced as if the lives of others depended on it. I knew that as I stepped forward to share my big idea on the TEDx platform, I had to trust God. It would be forever captured and available for the world to see thanks to social media. I felt like David with five stones called vulnerability, courage, determination, endurance, and perseverance. Empowered by the Holy Spirit, there was no stopping me now. The giant I faced was suicide. The big idea was to speak out and be used to demolish stigma by letting God call the broken to be mended by others who have already walked the road, healed with notable and evident divine work. Of course, you cannot preach from that platform, but the fire in my soul was lit!

The call to action was to every stakeholder: survivors that had lost loved ones, communities impacted by deaths from suicide, and those that attempted and survived but now live with a complex and compounded stigma. There was so much that could have—and did try to—set up or stir up wrong beliefs, but I had learned the art of doing a sound check. That is how I refer to testing the voices of self-talk. No more lies. I was taking the stage for someone that needs to discover hope and help. It was God's moment. Standing on the circular red rug reminded me that whether I stand, rise, or fall, it is all in the blood and in the name of Jesus. I could stand assured that I have been resurrected and made new.

I wish I could tell you it went as planned. It did go well, but the full message intended and prepared for a month was not delivered as I had hoped. Nonetheless, the Lord ordered my steps and drew out what was best[89] This platform is a one-time shot, and

---

87   Acts 3:17 Peter preached, "... I know that you acted in ignorance,"
88   Acts 17:30
89   See Appendix for the presentation.

once you present a big idea that idea cannot be given on another TEDx stage. The content must be new each time.

Fear and failure are inevitable parts of life. Success does not materialize without some measure of failure or fear. Both start early in life. Some fear is learned while some is innate. An infant learns to fear based on the pain associated when learning to hold things, crawl, and walk. Human resilience and determination to achieve is part of who you are by design. The small child will fail until he or she masters mobility, talking, and much more.

Fear can be healthy. Snakes cause concern in most people. When I encounter a slithering critter, it will die if it comes within striking distance of this gal. Whether a snake is venomous or not, the moment is not my concern. God put enmity between sapiens and serpents. I am thankful for such a healthy fear![90]

Fear is a God-given emotion. What we do with fear and failure varies, but the Bible gives remarkable guidance when it comes to both. There are countless failures, from Genesis to Revelation. Fear also abounds throughout Scripture sometimes as reverent awe and respect[91] and other times as a missing attribute that leads to behavior identified as godless,[92] yet other times it is an emotion subtly indicating we are caught in a spiritual snare from which there is an escape.[93]

God has made provision for every human failure. He never deviates from His holiness, Scripture, or His attributes. We are not

---

90 Genesis 3:15 And I will put enmity between you and the woman, and between your offspring and hers; he will crush your head, and you will strike his heel.

91 Psalm 27:1 The Lord is my light and my salvation; Whom shall I fear? The Lord is the defense of my life; Whom shall I dread?

92 2 Kings 17:32 To this day they do according to the earlier customs: they do not fear the Lord, nor do they follow their statutes or their ordinances or the law, or the commandments which the Lord commanded the sons of Jacob,

93 2 Timothy 1:7 For God has not given us a spirit of timidity, but of power and love and discipline.

consistent.[94] Some adopt portions of doctrine and reject others. God made provision for every human failure. He does not deviate. We are not consistent people. It does not matter what the sin, we have *all* sinned and fall short of God's glory.[95] We ought to live to please and serve God, not to please peers or appease peer pressures brought about by ignorant, stubborn, faulty human beings. Who do you seek to please? How do you navigate against social norms?

Stigma is the result of prejudice and discrimination directed by a group or large population. Suicide rocks everyone's world. There are many desired answers and often, they do not or will not come. When someone survives, the answers demanded and provided will not satisfy the need for individuals to reconcile and moreover, the moral injury that occurred results in public stigma compounded by self-stigma. Self-stigma happens when a person internalizes public attitudes and suffers negative consequences as a result. That may include self-imposed alienation, social isolation by others who are not sure how to navigate the pain, and shock of broken trust. It causes so much pain that this topic remains a very uneasy subject to bring up, even in ministry. To be sure, this topic elicits fear and failure. People fear not having skills to know what to do, how to respond, or where to point someone for adequate help, be it professional or volunteer. The failure on the part of ministry leaders is not placing a priority on honesty in these situations. Ministry hides behind fear and failure. This scenario forfeits so much spiritual territory where the enemy can and often does wreak more havoc. The church is often the first place people turn to in a crisis like this, and the church needs to step up like David to the giant of suicide, just like any other proverbial Goliath. Believers have what the world needs, and fear leads to failure.

---

94 2 Timothy 4:3-4 For the time will come when people will not put up with sound doctrine. Instead, to suit their own desires, they will gather around them a great number of teachers to say what their itching ears want to hear. They will turn their ears away from the truth and turn aside to myths.

95 Romans 3:23

What I learned concerning fear is that as an emotion, it stirs up every past event that has ever disappointed, let down, abandoned, hurt, or abused—both outwardly and inwardly. The only thing that kind of fear is right for is to present a wake-up call when you are gripped by it. The wake-up call is meant to drive you to your source of peace, power, and ever-present help.

Fear like that does not originate from God. It is fear that we can and must combat with the Spirit that God has given; His own Holy love, power, and a sound mind in the person of the Holy Spirit. Paul wrote to Timothy about a gift within; it is a gift you, as a follower of Christ, have too.

> *For this reason, I remind you to kindle afresh the gift of God which is in you through the laying on of my hands. For God has not given us a spirit of timidity (cowardice) but of power and love and discipline.*[96]

To become aware of what is available will stretch your personal faith because awareness unlocks the opportunity to trust God in ways that perhaps may not have been activated or exercised up to that point. You get to choose. Your choices lead to a new ripple effect or fuel an existing chain of events.

Confronting Failure

There are six points important to conquer failure:

1. Know that failure is a fact of life. It is not a way of life.
2. Accept forgiveness concerning failures and learn to forgive yourself.
3. Failure must be acknowledged to move past it. There is no shame in agreeing with God, and He already knows what happened. Be honest with yourself.
4. To arise from failure is to accept God's new mercy to start again with greater insight.

---

96 2 Timothy 1:6

5. It is imperative to apply lessons of failure toward success.
6. Lastly, do not judge others[97]

For every action there is an equal and opposite reaction. Failure repeated until mastered becomes success. Peter the disciple is notorious for speaking before thinking. So much so that Jesus rebuked him for speaking out reactively rather than giving a well-thought response.[98]

The motivation behind the speech determines whether it is reactive or not. A reaction tends to be emotionally driven with minimal thought of outcome versus a response with forethought. Ideally, we should consider the outcome before words are spoken. Hence the rebuke from Jesus to Peter. After three years of following Christ, Peter loved Jesus. In an emotional reaction, it would have been easy to fail to realize that his reaction was absurd; God could take care of Christ. He did not need human intervention. Thomas Edison, Albert Einstein, Abraham Lincoln, Walt Disney, and Alexander Graham Bell all lived with and pushed through one daunting failure after another. Rejection was also something that eventually resulted in building character, success, and impact.

To summarize, failure is not a person, it is an event. It is a lie and you are in complete disagreement with God when you embrace or believe any names called that label and refer to you or others as failures. Your identity is what God says it is.

TRIUMPH OVER TRAGEDY

The tragedy of sudden loss hits fiercely, without warning, and often the pain does not cease for long periods. Sudden death might happen due to a car crash fatality, line of duty death, or perhaps the result of criminal activity. Grief is something we all encounter at some point. How one navigates the inevitable pain of grief differs.

---

97 Adapted list from Dr. Jeremiah's list found in *Slaying The Giants In Your Life*.

98 Matthew 16:33 "But He turned and said to Peter, "Get behind Me, Satan! You are a stumbling block to Me; for you are not setting your mind on God's interests, but man's." See also Mark 8:33.

While there are studies and conclusions made about the phases and stages of grief, none factor the unique variables for each person impacted. No two sorrows are alike. Each loss is as unique as the relationship and individuals involved.

The grief brought on by the sudden loss from suicide is complicated by the unanswered questions. Unlike the death of a loved one from a homicide or other tragic deaths, the investigation for suicides only goes so far, and questions remain unanswered. Fear, desperation, and spiritual warfare accompany these unanswered questions. I refer to them as a trifecta of risk factors found in Scripture. God has communicated that you are not alone; He made provision and will help you to get through the most crushing tragedies of life.

Since our thoughts impact our emotions, they, in turn, affect the body. This can manifest in behaviors or lead to illness. We must also be aware that traumatic events can impact our faith. Simply put, to understand stress from a solid foundation of having the best opportunity to be transformed by traumatic events, we must look at Scriptures' precepts.

First, it is imperative to be mindful of what Scripture is clear about concerning the recorded suicides. Samson's life leading to his moment of death has indicators that he was in depressive circumstances. The other six deaths by suicide were acts of desperation. When we choose to accept and apply scripture to our lives, we are promised that our years will be many.[99]

No one is meant to journey this life alone. Sheep need a shepherd, and there is not a single lamb gone so astray that ought to ever go unnoticed or unattended by someone. Sheep have dense wool. When sheep lose footing while crossing a stream, their wool becomes saturated and creates a hazardous situation for the animal. It would be likened to times when it seems our world is turned upside down. The top-heavy position of drenched wool weighs it down, sending it belly up and feet in the air—not a pretty sight. Perhaps you can relate? The sheep are said to be cast down. To have

99 Proverbs 4:10

moments of sadness is one thing, but to be downcast has varied levels.

3 STAGES OF THE DOWNCAST

There are three stages in becoming downcast of which we must be aware.

The first and early stage can be accompanied by boredom, avoidance of family, anxiety, and sadness. This is moderate depression. It may manifest in changes to eating and sleep habits or a decline in performance at work or school. Concentration or decision making can become impaired. A decrease in future interests may also come up in conversation or in activity planning. This is apparent in the lament of Jeremiah as he remembers his affliction and wanderings, their impact and outcome. Evident in his cry, his soul is downcast.[100] The prophet is soul-sick. He did everything he could, he obeyed the Lord, and still, the people did their own thing. Those are reasonable sentiments under the circumstances, and we cannot just empathize we him, we must absorb the lesson to muster his courage by arming ourselves by taking our questions to scripture. People will use, "I don't know what to say in this situation," as an excuse, but have they asked scripture? Ask, "Why are you downcast? Why is your soul disturbed?" Then listen. Something weighs that soul down, like the sheep whose wool is saturated. Perhaps to you, the listener, the perspective resonates differently than it will to the downcast. However, the point is to be present, hear, empathize, and love the person in a hard place.

The second stage involves more considerable distress and may include full depression, self-pity, or mood swings paired with apathy or anger. The behavioral components can show up as withdrawal from family and friends, self-injury, physical problems including illness diagnosed as stress, self-medication, substance abuse, a decline in personal appearance, and patterned absences from school or work.

---

100 Lamentations 3:19-20

The Psalmist described it this way,

> *Trouble and distress have come upon or found me… Be merciful to me, LORD, for I am in distress; my eyes grow weak with sorrow, my soul and body are with grief."[101]*

This is a more advanced condition of soul distress. The life of Samson may hold unusual insight since he was predestined to be a Judge for Israel. God's plan for Samson was to begin Israel's deliverance from the Philistines. There is always opposition when God works in and through His people. Samson's life may have ended prematurely by the destruction of many Philistines. There are indisputable facts we do know about Samson, and these deserve attention. Samson must have had a rebellion or deviousness to his personality. Yet God used this for His purpose. Marrying a Timanite was not customary, yet God was at work. (Judges 14:4) He ate honey out of a dead animal and intentionally passed it along to his parents without telling them. This was a precise breach of the law. Samson experienced multiple betrayals; that of his wife telling the answer to his riddle. He reacted in anger and fled into isolation. It is reasonable to conclude the isolation as found in other similar instances are indicative to some sadness, perhaps depression, or grief.[102] When he returned for his wife, he learned about another betrayal. His bride was given to another man. In retaliation, Samson set the Philistine fields on fire. Then he suffered the betrayal of Delilah that cost him his eyesight, his strength, and his freedom. He was captive, broken, and yet determined to use what he had—his life—to destroy others. Do you see that as selfish? Samson's prayer speaks to his determination and grievance; the loss of sight.

O Lord God, please remember me and please strengthen me just this time, O God, that I may at once be avenged of the Philistines for my two eyes.[103]

---

101 Psalm 139:143 and Psalm 31:9
102 1 Kings 19:9 Elijah isolated when he was in woe, 2 Samuel 23:13 King David fled from Saul in despair.
103 Judges 16:28

His loss of vision is a crucial point to consider spiritually. Major loss can be a factor when times of desperation lead to suicidal thoughts. A mind in chaos becomes overcome by emotions, and consistent clarity in the mind is absent. An non-sober mind is at high risk for desperate actions. Samson was being humiliated as entertainment by his captors for all gathered to see. Proverbs tells us what happens when there is no vision—literally or metaphorically—people perish. Samson's situation presents evidence of a man in distress. His desire for vengeance for his eyes shows bitterness. His mind has enough clarity to pray with resolve and determination, boldly asking for the strength he knew would be fatal. Whatever his complete state of mind, soul, and spirit, he asked to die.

Others in scripture—Job, Jonah, Elijah, and Paul, for example—at some point, expressed a similar sentiment. Samson's suicide must be considered in its historical context. It was a time when Israel had no king, and everyone did what was right in his own eyes. That was evident even in Samson's life when he ate from and fed parents honey out of a carcass. Samson's suicide could possibly be the culmination of grief, desperation, and perhaps include depression. Given life events leading up to the moment, he had prayed to God and resolved to die. This suicide is documented at a time in history not far off describing society today; people have turned from God and do what seems right to them. The way of society ends in destruction.

The third stage or level of danger and risk of suicidal behavior is despair and warfare. For many, the assumption is that the situation or they themselves are hopeless. What may be perceived as an assumption of the loss of hope can be the chaos of spiritual warfare and lies from an enemy determined to kill off as many as possible. In my case, hope was not lost, I had placed my hope in the Lord. I became aware in a split second that I had acted contrary to what was holy within me. I was desperately crying out to the Lord to save me. Ultimately, He did. Still I spent three days suspended in a place of an abyss and on life support. A momentary consciousness while on life support resulted in a spiritual insight that I cannot explain. I knew that Satan did not want me alive. I also knew that God brought me through the unthinkable. I was livid, but not as one might think. I was furious and so confused how a child of God could have been led so far down a place of despair. All I can say is that I survived the cords of the grave that had coiled around me, and the snares of death confronted me.[104]

There is so much more to suicidal risks, care, and tragedies that we miss as a society. Suicide is not limited to a mental health crisis. It is a problem and the progression of humanity's depravity. Desperation is the most common denominator found in scripture. Momentary lapses of reason do not equate to mental illness. Everyone experiences painful thoughts. Even King David used words often relegated to the context of historical events. We must remember that scripture has near, present, and future fulfillment at the core of its truth. As long as we live in our bodies, we have an enemy that stalks people and seeks to destroy lives. He can torment the mind, body, and soul when we do not step back and consider how the return of Christ escalates evil in so many ways. The crisis of death by suicide should be met with no less compassion than when a widow or orphan encounters the trauma of loss.

A mental health referral without a continuum of spiritual and pastoral care is placing eternity at risk, and this is a risk that ministry leaders should not be willing to take. There is a way that seems right, and the end leads to destruction. A Christian therapist who counsels from a place of faith versus therapists who happen to be Christian, yet provide therapy from the foundation of evidence-based theory, will have different client outcomes. The heart, soul, and a person's beliefs impact recovery and process. Without hesitation, ministries must reevaluate the situations in which they are serving. An accumulation of wounded souls going through other life-altering events is on the frontline of situations that can lead to a more complicated situation. Perhaps tragic crises could be caught before traumatic events or preventable death devastates more lives. Education is required to equip those serving in ministry,

104 2 Samuel 22:6

and ministries must realize the critical role it has in helping those in and outside the church.

On any given day, statistics indicate that for every one hundred people, six percent of adolescents seventeen and under have thought about suicide. Twenty percent are worried about someone who is at risk or shows signs of suicide.[105] Most are afraid to ask about it because they believe erroneously that asking will plant a seed. As many as thirty-three percent have experienced the loss of or know someone who has attempted suicide. One in two people is impacted in some way by suicide. We are living in times not too different than when the Old Testament Law was given. There is no judgment to point out that Leviticus commanded God's people not to cut or mark their body for dead. I have found that every tattoo has a story, and so often there is pain behind the story. Those too young to get inked are silently expressing sorrow in a way similar to the same passage. Self-harm is rampant among youth. Some therapists refer to the behaviors as non-suicidal self-injury. While the behavior may indicate that the mind and heart are sick or desperate, that person is not overlooked by the Lord. He is near the brokenhearted and crushed in spirit. If things of the world that impact the body of believers are not dealt with in the church and as outreach, we are no better than unbelievers.

HOW DOES FEAR IMPACT SUICIDE IN SCRIPTURE?

Fear, as it relates to suicide, happens in the extreme. Fear that drives one to consider taking a life does not originate from a holy place, yet we, being human, experience it at varying levels.

> *Fear and trembling come upon me, and horror has overwhelmed me.*[106]

---

105 Suicide statistics at a glance fact sheet https://www.cdc.gov/
    violenceprevention/pdf/suicide-datasheet-a.pdf
106 Psalm 55:5

> *The fear of man brings a snare, but he who trusts in the Lord will be exalted.*[107]

There are six aspects of fear evident and present in the death of King Saul who feared torture upon military defeat. Pain can amplify fear as well as convolute an otherwise lucid mind.[108] The armor-bearer feared abandonment and also faced abuse and torture.[109] Ahithophel met the repercussions of having started a mutiny against King David. His death was not in as much haste as the others. He took time to get things in order and then ended his life.[110] King Abimelech feared the humiliation of his reputation. He would rather die than to have had it said that a woman killed him.[111] Full-blown pride and fear are a lethal combination. Zimri was a wanted man and feared retaliation and torched his palace while he was in it. Such desperation would have destroyed the body so there were no remains to display after his death. Finally, the Philippian jailer feared severe punishment when it was discovered that the prison doors and chains had all opened. Paul intervened in this potential suicide.

The Bible repeatedly indicates that desperation can lead to rash, hasty, and fatal actions. Suicide is typically a secondary response to a deeper unseen problem that has its core rooted in some sin; be it committed against or by the person. It can also be on account of generational strongholds. The person bears a lack of resilience skills and discipleship, so they know how to take up the full armor of God and use the Word of God to pierce the darkness.

---

107 Proverbs 29:25
108 1 Chronicles 10:4
109 1 Chronicles 10:5
110 2 Samuel 17:23
111 Judges 9:54

Post-Trauma Growth

Fearfully and Wonderfully Made

I will give thanks to You, for I am fearfully and wonderfully made;
Wonderful are Your works, and my soul knows it very well.
— Psalm 139:14

I decisively sought transformation following my suicide attempt. The impact of Post-Traumatic Stress Disorder including depression, anxiety, and chronic migraines hit me full force. I utilized counselors and sought help like never before from power I had trusted in far less than I realize. The change that I found and pursued was rooted in faith and a sincere, desperate desire. The result over many years is Post Trauma Growth. The result was personal Post-Trauma Growth (PTG). The growth came as the result of what I learned about myself, God's provision, and that I sought to learn more about post-trauma stress to help others. On a journey through post-trauma growth, I discovered things that grew my intimacy to my Savior and Lord, Jesus Christ.

A NARSAD[112] study looked exclusively at women with depression or PTSD. All of the PTSD patients involved were women who had experienced intimate partner violence. They had not taken any psychiatric medication for at least three weeks before testing,

---

112 The Brain & Behavior Research Foundation is a nonprofit 501(c)(3) organization that funds mental health research. It was originally called the National Alliance for Research on Schizophrenia & Depression or the acronym for that, NARSAD.

making it less likely the study's findings stem from medication use. Within this population, depression severity correlated with fewer connections between the amygdala and three other brain regions. The dorsolateral prefrontal cortex is important for evaluating risk and moral decisions. The anterior cingulate cortex is associated with decision making as well as regulating emotion and physiological processes, including heart rate. The anterior insula helps build the basis for all subjective experiences of the body likely including the emotional experience.

In short, emotions can lead to poor decisions. Poor decisions can manifest behaviorally in such ways as to contradict logic, rationale, and affecting one's reasoning to make decisions. We all have emotions, a brain, and a gut. Some call the stomach a second brain as it often functions to produce what some refer to as a sense, or gut feeling, that something is not right. While the gut or stomach is not a moral compass, somehow, we have an innate ability to sense danger. Trauma impairs that.

Humans are capable of doing things that even they cannot explain when mentally and situationally overloaded. What we've gained in knowledge, wisdom, and insight is marred by the chaos. At times the emotionally flooded mind overrides gut feelings because thoughts become a belief, albeit temporary, and they can be so compelling that actions are emotionally reactive rather than logically responsive.

It is important to understand the difference between a reaction and response. Each behavior originates from the brain, yet neither is triggered by the same cerebral section. Reactions are innate behaviors that may be learned or are instinctive. In trauma, behaviors can take on survival traits such as fight, flight, or freeze. These are reactions similar to that seen in reptiles. To the contrary, the mammalian brain response operates cognitively differently. Reactions are most often directed by the 911 operating center of the brain known as the amygdala.

Responses, on the other hand, involve the hypothalamus, hippocampus, amygdala, and cingulate cortex. This is the center of our motivation, emotions, and memory. This also includes the neocortex that enables language, abstraction, reasoning, and planning.

In trauma, the pea-sized pituitary gland releases a surge of fluids that alter all brain functions and how the mind primarily functions. If you ask someone, "What were you thinking?" following a trauma, there is a good possibility that the person answers in a less than satisfactory manner. The answer may be lacking because they are too young to understand, or they are in a place of survival or experiencing that reptile brain function mentioned earlier. A word of caution when questioning someone, you cannot judge their behavior from a place of logic. The one asking will be less than satisfied with most responses given. For the one questioned, there are times that a question can impose shame. Emotions can be spawned by questions. I believe a better question than "Why?" is to ask "How?" How, in light of what makes no sense, can the present situation make an improved difference for the person's future and for others? If the world can become better for one person because of tragedy, then the chance to impact the world for better exists.

The same study found that "while reduced amygdala connections were linked to depression, more severe anxiety symptoms meant increased connections between the amygdala and other brain regions. Those regions included the ventromedial prefrontal cortex, associated with fear-based and social aspects of decision making, and the subgenual anterior cingulate cortex thought to regulate diffuse brain areas, especially those needed for processing sadness."[113]

Simply put, what we dwell on literally fuels a neurological network that releases a host of enzymes and hormones that are further altered by the thoughts that repeat in the mind as self-talk that can lead to rumination. The brain is changed by one's thoughts and beliefs. Negative thoughts come with a high cost. As Dr. Caroline Leaf puts it: "To not take thoughts captive compromises far more than mental. The repercussions contribute to poor health. Toxic thoughts can lead to depressive thoughts that impact our immune

113 https://www.bbrfoundation.org/connections-brain%E2%80%99s-emotion-center-tied-symptoms-depression-and-ptsd

system setting off inflammatory responses that left unattended can escalate to hardening of arteries and cardiovascular disease." (Switch On Your Brain p.74) The very nature of physiological changes in our brain is continuously proving that when the mind is fixed on what is true, whatever is honorable, whatever is right, whatever is pure, whatever is lovely, whatever is of good repute—then it is transformed. The very thoughts we fixate on or that the emotions we react to are a behavioral by-product of either how fearful we are in a given moment or how fearfully we are focused on who is indeed in control of that instant.

These findings paint a picture of the amygdala as a driving factor behind negative symptoms in both PTSD and depression. Depression symptoms reflect reduced connections, and anxiety symptoms reflect increased connections. Treatments might be improved, the researchers say, by targeting these brain networks for different symptoms and continuing to study overlap between PTSD and major depressive disorder. The researchers note that future work should explore whether these findings reflect long-lasting traits of people with PTSD and depression, rather than temporary moods brought on by their conditions. Indeed the need for further research should include data with a more holistic approach, given that man is mind, body, and soul/spirit. To dismiss any part of man's make-up is to negate how mental wellness and health are linked to the spiritual and to what is believed. God does not prove science, science proves God Almighty and His design of the human body. The capabilities of the Designer and the blueprint for we (the designed) are contained in Scripture. Time and again, science affirms what waits to be revealed to anyone willing to grow in wisdom.

Isn't it fascinating that what the mind cannot comprehend it sometimes limits itself from learning to receive by development and transformation? The beauty of this conundrum is that we all have the choice and opportunity to grow.

While reduced amygdala connections were linked to depression, the researchers found that more severe anxiety symptoms meant increased connections between the amygdala and other brain regions: the ventromedial prefrontal cortex, associated with fear-based and social aspects of decision making, and the subgenual anterior cingulate cortex, thought to regulate diffuse brain areas, especially those needed for processing sadness.

What I learned about the way we are designed, and the neurobiological function of the brain, is that post-trauma growth is not only possible, it is plausible. When one is willing, supported, and able to focus we have an opportunity to grow volitionally. That said, it is more difficult to unlearn patterned behavior or habits than it is to learn something new. The effort and dedication are worth it and far outweigh the pain of suffering in a cycle of brokenness.

The brain and fullness of mind are most capable of receiving and experiencing growth when all brain function is clear and in homeostasis. It is capable of being transformed by the renewing of mind: thoughts, feelings, beliefs, and actions.

Forgive the awkwardness of grammar, but there are times that reading and re-reading aloud brings us to wrestle with what the mind automatically rejects for any number of reasons. In this case, the grammar may act as a foe. It comes down to how does one "be?" Scripture says not to *be c*onformed to this world, but *be* transformed by the renewing of your mind, so that you may prove what the will of God is, that which is good and acceptable and perfect."[114] One must grapple with the result desired. A good business planner would urge that a solid plan begins with the end in mind. To navigate in the will of God, one must "be." The word be is a verb requiring much attention. It also connotes one's disposition. *To be* is a disposition of availability and receptivity. If I am not to be conformed, I must be aware that unlearning will be required. If I am to be transformed, I must accept what the directive is and what it is not. First, the directive is not that I do the work of transformation. Transformation is not in me to accomplish. I cannot see the inner workings of the body, so I must simply be available and in agreement that the work of transformation is yet to be done in

114 Romans 12:2

all areas of me. Second, a transformation is available to receive. To receive all that transformation in myself, is to be renewed. To glean the greatness of Romans 12:2, I must align with all that the be verb entails; past, present, and future me. For example, I was conformed to brokenness. I am now redeemed and released to become all God's plan is for me. I will continue to seek growth as my Lord continues to perfect in me all that is corrupt. I can be my best in Christ. One must be transformed, be renewed, and most difficult of all—just "be." He does what is unseen to the individual who has submitted to His ability in our own disability.

Here is the good news: There is a plan and a purpose for you. The plan originates with the Creator, God, whose blueprint is designed so that you may thrive. You are never as alone as you may feel. We have an enemy that seeks to kill every hope, steal every dream, and destroy us by attacking our identity and image. God, on the other hand, has come to give us unshakable identity and rescue us from every corrupt thing in this world. The enemy is good at what he does because he is a liar. He is sly in approach because chaos disproportionately is fueled by a running dialogue of what we believe. Our mind is a battleground. What we think and believe subsequently feeds our emotions. Emotions are supposed to drive us to respond with the Spirit of the living God Almighty who loves you. He is always in control of what is beyond our ability. We are human; we have limits.

God is infinite, He is all-powerful. He is for you, not against you. Beliefs can change. The choice is ours to grow like Christ in every way: wisdom, stature, and knowledge. Chronologically, our bodies mature and grow. We don't choose those changes, but we do decide to grow in wisdom and knowledge. We have the freedom to pursue growth and personal development continually for all our days. Past performance is not a one-hundred percent predictor of future realized potential. Anyone can be transformed. It does not have to take a traumatic event. Although trauma and failure are incidents that may have a significant impact, they should not be allowed to have a detrimental impact on how you view yourself or

God. We choose the effect any tragedy will have on how we view ourselves or God in the long run.

God never wastes a hurt when we seek to be strengthened by the Healer. God desires that we pursue His plan, that we partner with Him to co-create our lives from His blueprint so that we prosper and are reconciled into eternal perfection. Even in sorrow and suffering, there is a purpose. While God may not be the cause of trauma or tragedy, He will use it for and in his plan.

We are so wonderfully made. King David beautifully wrote about how amazing our bodies are designed. He was blown away at such revelation. We need not give fear a place of residence in who we are, other than to revere an awesome God. Lastly, fear is not a grip we were given, it is an emotion to prompt us to be alert and respond in love, power, and with a sound mind. What the mind is willing to receive and conceive, Christ is able to achieve in His sons and daughters. Believe this and please do not lose sight that you are created in His image. You are who God's Word says you are.

Preparing for Battle

Tear down the Walls

> *For though we live in the world, we do not wage war as the world does. The weapons we fight with are not the weapons of the world. On the contrary, they have divine power to demolish strongholds.*
>
> — 2 Corinthians 10:3-5

The Lord loves to destroy forces and fortresses. He is the breaker of strongholds, the Deliverance from captivity, and He loves setting His children free. He does so in ways that are not familiar to our ideas and does not act in the way the world tells us it ought to be.

"For my thoughts are not your thoughts, neither are your ways my ways," declares the Lord.

— Isaiah 55:8

Things God directs us to do often seems absurd to us and even more so to those around us. God loves us in one way: completely. We humans give Him varying depths of love and commitment. God's game plan and blueprint are of an eternal world, time, and space. There are limitations to our ability to have a full understanding.[115]

The most significant victories come when we find ourselves overpowered, overwhelmed, wholly intimidated, outnumbered, and outmuscled. It is then that we come to a broken and humble realization that we can either trust God and travail in truth or die trying to survive in our failing strength.

When God fights a battle through us, it is against the odds and without regard to appearance. When we posture in the name for which we desire to bring fame, the name above all names, everything changes. When we strive to perform and preserve personal reputation or to keep up appearances, we fight in the flesh and diminishing strength.

Consider Joshua. His assignment was to march, scream, and blow a horn. How perplexing must it have been to receive these as the only instructions for victory. March around Jericho once a day for six days with seven priests carry trumpets in front of the ark, and on the seventh day, march around the city seven times, then have the priests blow the horns? Nothing about that fits a battle strategy yet, the battle was assured.

The secret of embracing such a strategy is demonstrated in Joshua 5:13-15 "Now when Joshua was near Jericho, he looked up and saw a man standing in front of him with a drawn sword in his hand. Joshua went up to him and asked, 'Are you for us or for our enemies?' 'Neither,' he replied, 'but as commander of the army of the Lord I have now come.' Then Joshua fell facedown to the

---

115 Proverbs 3:5-6

ground in reverence, and asked him, 'What message does my Lord have for his servant?' The commander of the Lord's army replied, 'Take off your sandals, for the place where you are standing is holy.' And Joshua did so."

First, it is imperative to recognize that God's plan may involve the risk of ridicule. It is sure to require vulnerability, and it will exert every faith muscle a willing servant has.

Second, realize that to the human mind, your opponent only appears impossible to defeat. This is not reality. When the walls come down, victory is the reward.

HOW TO BRING DOWN WALLS

1. Have a clear understanding of God's plan. Clarity does not often come within our limited knowledge. It may not fit our understanding. Trust in the trustworthy.

2. Before carrying out God's instruction, you must know His plan. He is for you, not against you. Culture may say this is not a time to give up ground and you should stand your ground. God instructs us to forgive others. He teaches us whose ground it is. (Psalm 50:12) He promises to impart what is ours to steward. Others may say that you should exercise personal rights. God's instruction is to deny yourself.

3. There must be complete cooperation with God's strategy. No adding to, vearing from, or altering of God's instruction.

4. By faith, obedience leads to victory. (Hebrews 11:30) "By faith the walls of Jericho fell after the army had marched around them for seven days."

BATTLE PRINCIPLES

1. The battle faced is not difficult because of size or circumstances. It is difficult because it feels impossible. The odds should not be denied or ignored, but trust that God is greater than circumstances appear. The counsel of doubt should not be given an audience or mental real estate when it is contrary to who God is.

Listen to what the Lord says to you. Confirm what you discern by His word, in who He is, and by His nature.

2. The plan you are to follow is not a struggle because it is complicated or confusing. It is a struggle because it seems a strange and unfamiliar way to win a war. To pray, to trust, or refuse to have our reputation involved is countercultural. Beware of those that want to hold you back or give advice and counsel that is contrary to God's instruction.

3. The victory needed is not accomplished in personal strength, aptitude, or intellect. The triumph comes through the wisdom of God and others will not get it. If you happen to be close to someone when the battle is won God's way, give Him the credit. Be a good steward of the victory.

Joshua 6:27 "So the Lord was with Joshua, and his fame spread throughout the land."

God won the battle. God brought the wall down. Joshua obeyed by marching and shouting, and his fame spread throughout the land. Why? The world deeply desires a conqueror, a victor, a mighty leader. Joshua's stewardship of glory was to point the people back to God, just as it is with our testimony.

Joshua had no strength to move a single stone. He set aside all human temptation to manipulate and maneuver God's plan to come out looking like a hero. He determined that obedience and honoring God's plan, regardless of how others may view it, was the best option. In the results, all glory belongs to God.

God did the impossible, and his servant got fame. We are strong, and there is every temptation to get stronger. We are reasonably smart and educated with every temptation to rely on personal intellect. We are personable and have every temptation to be impressed with this person or that person. Be impressed with the Lord.

CONCLUSION

We will face trials of so many kinds. The church and its people have all authority and empowerment to lead the charge to be the message of hope that people in the world need.

As end times escalate in the coming of Christ, the battles faced will intensify. I am thankful Scripture addresses crisis response so adequately. Provision by design is always in place regardless of how difficult circumstances may get.

God's best for us may not always be easy, but God's plan is in our best interest. He has provided a way out of every temptation. It is up to us to choose the way that draws us closer to Him. As believers, it is up to us to continue to grow and humbly serve others no matter what arises as a challenge. No one was created to do life alone. I believe that the greatest tragedy is when God's people back away from engaging in an assault on a fellow neighbor. May we humble ourselves, learn by the guidance of the Holy Spirit, and serve courageously.

Appendix I

Complete Interview Questions for Pastors

Approximately how many active members does this church have?

Does the church have a denomination affiliation?

What is your highest level of education?

Do you have any specialized training, continuing education, certifications or accreditations beyond the last degree attained?

If so, what area of specialty?

Have you or anyone on staff ever participated in any form of trauma or crisis stress management seminars?

THE FOLLOWING QUESTIONS ARE SPECIFIC AND WILL USE TERMS WITH THE FOLLOWING MEANING:

Suicide survivor: is an individual personally impacted and left to process the grief and death of a loved one that died by suicide.

Attempt Survivor is an individual that acted to attempt suicide and did not die.

Postvention is defined as actions taken to help suicide survivors cope with the death of someone that died by suicide.

Postvention may also include ministry to attempt survivors coping beyond their action and moving toward healing.

Are you a suicide or suicide attempt survivor?

Is anyone in your family an attempt survivor?

As a minister, have you personally faced an incident of a church member or family member of a congregant that would be considered a suicide survivor? Traumatic or sudden loss?

How do you view your role to suicide survivors?

What is your Theological conclusion concerning death by suicide?

How do you minister in the wake of death by suicide?

Within this ministry's leadership, is there a level of willingness to provide postvention care to suicide survivor families during bereavement?

Considering that all grief is not the same, and many must move beyond traumatic events of various kinds. What if any ministry is there for families that face a traumatic loss?

Is suicide trauma a form of a proverbial "elephant" that leaders or member affected pull away, withdraw or shrink back from ministering to readily?

In general, what are your thoughts about ministry to suicide survivors as a leader?

We are not just referring to suicide alone but could include homicide or sudden/unexpected deaths. Is traumatic loss a challenge this congregation could be better equipped to respond to?

Is it openly known by congregants that there is clergy help in deaths of traumatic nature?

Do you believe clergy, in general, is helpful in such situations or have others expressed concern, harm, hurt, or damage despite the best intentions?

Does church policy or procedures clearly state leadership expectations and how to handle a family in such a crisis as suicide survival? Traumatic event survival?

Have you ever been suicidal? (at what time in life)

Would you say that as a pastor you are prepared, minimally prepared, ill-prepared, or uncomfortable to minister people grieving a death by suicide?

Is there anyone in your church that ministers specifically to families grieving death by suicide?

What if any specific preparation has clergy or volunteer leaders had for crisis or traumatic response as a ministry?

Is this ministry open to ministering to the increasing epidemic of suicide?

Is this ministry open to ministering to attempt survivors?

Are survivors ministered to within this ministry or referred elsewhere be it to mental health professionals or another ministry?

Are mental health professional referrals faith-based or mainstream therapists?

Do you have a list of referring therapists or facilities readily available to those in need?

Are your leaders and volunteers equipped to minister in the event of a traumatic crisis within the community?

If you could see a change in the church concerning trauma or suicide postvention ministry, what would that look like?

Does this church ministry utilize crisis-trained chaplains or have or designated organizations that would be called upon if there was a need to activate CRISIS RESPONSE MINISTRY?

Is this ministry prepared with an action plan for its role in immediate community response? Please explain what would transpire.

Would you be interested in making available to your church or community a 2-day course in how to minister in the wake of the traumatic crisis?

Would you have interest in a 2-day seminar covering suicide intervention, prevention, and postvention?

How many years have you served in ministry?

How many members would you say are part of your congregation?

Interview Questions for Chaplains

What is your chaplaincy specialty? Explain your role.

Are you utilized within your church to minister for special skills you have obtained minister to those in crisis?

Have you offered such crisis ministry to your congregation?

How was it received?

Who ministers to you?

What has been your experience when you start to share with someone in ministry not equipped to endure the unique suffering of crisis ministry?

What points of insight do you share?

Have you offered to minister to other churches?

How was that received?

What do you see as room for improvement concerning chaplaincy?

INTERVIEW QUESTIONS FOR STAKEHOLDERS

Are you a survivor of crisis trauma incident, traumatic loss, a suicide attempt, or death? At the time of the event, were you an active member of a church or faith-based ministry?

At the time or after the incident, did you let someone in ministry know about your situation?

What kind of ministry was available?

Did you find that ministry helpful?

Was there anything that was not helpful?

Did a representative of any ministry volunteer, church staff, or clergy follow up with you over any period? If so for about how long?

Would it have been helpful to have a "ministry of presence" or any other form of support during the first year of your grief?

Would that have been accepted, helpful, or received?

How much time would seem reasonable to you for persons in ministry to periodically touch base with your need for ministry? (Ex: after but not before the first year was over)

What boundaries to grief or trauma ministry would you consider helpful?

What if any support was available?

Did you call upon any support system? Which?

Did you look to spiritual support? What was your experience in doing so?

What would have been most supportive of you or your family?

What would you advise church leaders to consider in light of what you have gone through at this point?

TRAUMATIC INCIDENT

What incident occurred?

Did you find or learn of any type of ministry available for your unique situation? What?

Was it a referral outside your current spiritual "family" or place of worship?

What meant a lot to you after the crisis?

Does anything stand out that indeed blessed, impacted, or helped you?

Were there any unmet expectations of support from your spiritual home base "Church?"

What if anything meant most to you about your faith community after the crisis?

TRAUMATIC LOSS

What was the cause of the traumatic loss?

Did you find or learn of any type of ministry available within your congregation for your unique situation? What?

Was it a referral outside your current spiritual "family" or place of worship?

What meant a lot to you after the crisis?

Did others reach out to you?

Clergy or laity?

Does anything stand out that indeed blessed, impacted, or helped you?

Were there unmet expectations of support from your spiritual home base "Church?"

What if anything meant most to you about your faith community after the crisis?

SUICIDE SURVIVORS

Are you the survivor of a loved one that died by suicide or are you the survivor of attempted suicide?

Did you find or learn of any type of ministry available for your unique situation? What?

Were you referred outside your spiritual "family" or place of worship for help and
support?

Was there a willingness from clergy or volunteers to support you during and after the incident/loss?

What if anything meant most to you about your faith community after the crisis?

Does anything stand out that indeed blessed, impacted, or helped you?

Were there any unmet expectations of support from your spiritual home base "Church?"

Are there others in the immediate or extended family that have either died by or attempted suicide?

Are you or anyone in your family a suicide attempt survivor?

Have you ever been offered specific ministry concerning your traumatic event?

Were there people that know or knew your situation that reached out as any means of support?

How did you find people to respond upon learning of your tragedy?

What kind of support was available to help you afterwards?

Were there efforts made to be present at critical times after the situation?

What if anything changed regarding your involvement with church or faith-based congregations?

Based on your situation and pain, what recommendations can you offer for those in ministry either as staff or a volunteer that should be considered for others in similar situations to you?

What would you tell someone in your situation to do that helped you most?

Any additional feedback that people and leaders in churches should know about?

As difficult as the tragedy was, has anything positive resulted that might not have had that pain never changed your life?

Appendix II

9 Step Emergency Size Up

Gather Facts. What happened? How many people appear to be involved? What is the current situation?

Assess and communicate the damage. Try to determine what has happened, what is happening now, and how bad things can really get.

Consider probabilities. What is likely to happen? What could happen through cascading events?

Assess your own situation. Are you in immediate danger? Have you been trained to handle the situation? Do you have the equipment that you need?

Establish priorities. Are lives at risk? Can you help? Remember, life safety is the first priority!

Make decisions. Base your decisions on the answer to steps one through five and by the priorities that you established.

Develop a plan of action. Develop a plan that will help you accomplish your priorities. Simple plans may be verbal, but more complex plans should always be written.

Take action. Execute your plan, documenting deviations and status changes so that you can report the situation accurately to first responders.

Evaluate progress. At intervals, evaluate your progress in accomplishing the objectives in the plan of action to determine what is working and what changes you may have to make to stabilize the situation.

Appendix III

Capitalization use with acronym use is intentional.

September 22nd, 2009, I briefly awoke on life support. Three days earlier, I attempted suicide.

On a journey through Post Trauma Growth, I discovered things about fear and failure that now contribute to suicide prevention. Language and reactions surrounding suicide need to change. Post-Traumatic Stress is not limited to negative life experience. In fact, it can elevate you to a stronger and better way of life through P.T.G.

Post-Trauma Growth or P.T.G. is personal development that intentionally unlearns what is damaging and learns how to be more mentally resilient and potentially available to help others with similar trauma.

The Center for Disease Control reported more than forty-four thousand deaths by suicide in the United States with a global death toll of eight-hundred thousand in 2018. Suicide is the 2nd leading cause of death in students fifteen to twenty-four years old. It is estimated that for every death by suicide, thirty attempts survive. Because Many fear the subject, we miss opportunities that could be the difference between life and death. Together, we can change this.

As a kid, I played a game to race barefooted across a field full of stickers and thorns and not to get stuck. The first person to get stuck lost. The winner typically celebrated success as the others felt the impact of loss and painfully removed stickers and splinters.

I tell you this because we are all naturally quick to react to success, fear, and failure. Reactions can miss the fact that suicide has resulted in a fatal cycle of hurt people transferring hurt to other people. That is the result of all suicide.

To respond is to take prepared actions and use words that lead toward the goal of saving lives.

Using 3 Acronyms for the word F.E.A.R., I will share changes that can impact outcomes.

Fear can impact what we do or don't do. We react by fight, flight, or fear can cause a person to freeze in shock, panic, pain, or chaos when False Evidence Appears Real. In my darkest moments, fear like that almost cost me my life.

We must all learn not to succumb to lies believed in the chaos of pain.

Survival altered my perspective of fear and gripped me. While I had some support; more people were reacting in flight than present and available. I can't blame them. My own shock led to moments of also wanting to Forget Everything And Run into isolation and from rejection I got from others in pain.

Social isolation can increase the perception of being alone in a fight, and it is a fight for a life worth preserving. No one should fight alone. Growth does not happen in a comfort zone. It takes vulnerability, courage, determination, endurance, and perseverance. These are the pure grit that helps us push through a situation. Post Trauma Growth is uncomfortable, but so is having a baby and having done both, believe me pressing into this pain is also worth the gain. The most significant benefit is fewer lives compromised to suicide!

Post-Trauma Growth is key to suicide prevention.

It interrupts downward mental spiraling, compels transformed living, and is an effective means of peer support for others struggling through their recovery.

It builds peer connections that foster strength like nothing else can.

A Few More Things that help demolish stigma. If you know someone that attempted and survived; show up! Be part of a positive support system; Being present speaks volumes. Twenty billion people from ten to sixty-four years old survived an attempt in 2018. That is not failure! Not doing anything different about this is!

A little bit more about language. People do not succeed or fail at suicide. They either die or attempted and survived. Either way, it shatters lives. Success is not in death, it is in what will be done differently by all of us. The phrase "completed suicide" is harmful. That phrase amidst chaotic thoughts is toxic. The expression and word "completed" should not be used in any context of suicide!

We need a greater focus on building resilience. By the way, when did you gain resilience skills to maintain the one mind that no one wants to lose?

Never before crossing a line, I did not think possible of me had I considered failure an opportunity. Now, alive, I celebrate the fact that failure is an event, and it is not now, nor will it ever be; my identity.

Serving as a crisis responder for more than twenty years, I can tell you that peer support saves lives. Trauma stress is a risk we all encounter on some level.

No one wants P.T.S.D., yet, tragic events, including natural disasters and mass shootings, have a residual impact. Responders, military, our elderly, 9 & 10 yr. Olds, should not die by suicide. Still, it happens at an alarming rate. Outcomes can change through Post Trauma Growth.

When I was eighteen years old, my brother, a friend and I went rafting. It was going great until our raft was swept into a flash flood. The catastrophe that happened next because the life vests were in the bottom of the boat instead of on us meant that when the boat went over a submerged bridge, the undertow sucked the raft under as we were ejected helplessly into surging water. Thankfully we were swept onto an island.

My friend was having an asthma attack. Her inhaler was on the other side of the raging water. I plunged into the chest-deep raging water - that pulled and tugged back and forth, but I returned with that inhaler.

Everything in me told me that not doing something was fatal. The same is true for us all concerning suicide prevention. For me, not speaking up; it is not optional. For us, any fear that leads to no change at all is detrimental. We are all stakeholders!

When we each bravely choose to embrace a new perspective of fear. You will be ready to join me to Face Everything And Rise. That is when the current of change begins.

In a similar way that we are all touched by suicide negatively, Post Trauma Growth stands to benefit everyone positively. Post-Trauma Growth can change outcomes, and it is not limited to suicide.

We must be willing to look in the mirror and face our own fear and failure. Stigma & Shame? Don't be part of the problem, be a solution. Casting Judgement & Discrimination are counterproductive to saving lives. Gossip & labels are a careless and damaging use of words that rip open, invisible wounds.

To Quote Albert Einstein, "Insanity is doing the same thing over and over again and expecting different results." I challenge you to consider that not doing anything over and over again, is negligent. Suicide is preventable. Now is the time to move from quiet grief and desperation and boldly respond to STOP the SUICIDE crisis. Together we can Face Everything And Rise to make a difference!

Appendix IV

How Trauma Stress Can Manifest: Body Talk That Is Asking For Help

The material on the following pages is formatted for easy duplication and with permission to reprint, We are only as effective as the resources we implement to maintain health and wellness.

The charts provided on the next four pages are available as a PDF file, 8.5" x 11", for you to print or for easier reading. You can find the PDF for preview or download on this book's catalog page, https://www.energiondirect.com/product/love-me-to-life, or by pointing your smartphone camera at the QR code below.

How Trauma Stress Can Manifest: Body Talk That Is Asking For Help

The following numbers are made available so that no one suffers in silence. Your unseen pain is worthy of self care and recovery.
National Suicide Hotline 800-784-2433, TEXT 741 741 "help" "(Blue" for LEO's, "RED" for Figherfighters this will route you to peer support)

PHYSICAL	MENTAL	EMOTIONAL	BEHAVIOR	SPIRITUAL
Fatigue	Blame someone	Anxiety	Change activity	Irritated by religions platitudes
Muscle tension	Poor Attention	Guilt/ survivor guilt	Withdrawal	Question basic beliefs
Chest Pains* (see a Dr.)	Poor Decisions	Denial	Emotional outburst	Withdraw from place of worship
Difficulty Breathing* (see a Dr.)	Poor concentration	Emotional shock	Suspicious	Uncharacteristic religious involvement
Elevated BP* (see a Dr.)	Alertness lower / raised	Fear	Change in communication	Sudden turn from God
Thirst	Memory problems	Uncertainty	Restlessness	Familiar faith practice is empty
Headaches	Hyper Vigilance	Emotional control problems	Alcohol use increase	Belief that God is powerless
Vision Problems	or awareness of surroundings	Depression	Appetite loss or increase	Loss of meaning and purpose
Vomiting	Poor problem solving ability	Powerful outbursts of emotions	Acting out	Feeling distant
Grinding Teeth	Poor abstract thinking	Apprehension	Nonspecific body complaints	Anger at clergy
Weakness	Impaired thinking	Overwhelmed	Hyper alert to environment	Belief that God is not in control
Dizziness	Nightmares	Intense anger	Intensified startling response	God does not care
Profuse sweating	Flashbacks	Irritability	Intensified startling response	Belief that failed God you
Chills	Impaired focus	Agitation	Pacing	Anger at God
Shock Symptoms*	Thinking thoughts or emotions are "crazy"	Severe panic	increase /decreased sexual activity	Moral compromise

AGES 1-5	AGES 1-5	AGES 1-5	AGES 1-5	AGES 1-5
PHYSICAL	MENTAL	EMOTIONAL	Regressive BEHAVIOR	SPIRITUAL
indigestion	Needs consistency	Anxious / Nervous	Thumb sucking	May want to attend Church
Bowel control	Reassurance that they are not alone	Irritable	Bed wetting	May talk more about prayer
Bladder control - urgent urination or wetting pants	Renforcement of support system	Hyperactive	Animal fears	Withdraw from church mates
Difficulty Breathing* (see a Dr.)	Looking for reassurance in actions and words	Shock / nonverbal or withdrawing when spoken to	Suspicious / Increased fear of strangers	Questions about God
overeating/ frequency of eating	Watchful for evidence that caregivers is trustworthy	Fear of animals Short attention span	Afraid of the dark	Angry about Familiar faith concepts
Vomiting	Needs affirmation of stability feel safe.	Speech difficulty	Restlessness	May think that God is powerless
AGES 5-11	AGES 5-11	AGES 5-11	AGES 5-11	AGES 5-11
Sleep disruptions / disordered	Needs reassurance of support system	Powerful outbursts of emotions	Acting out contrary to age	May ask for prayer more frequently
Grinding Teeth day or night	Poor abstract thinking	School phobia /apprehensions	Crying whimpering	Anger at clergy
Weak / lethargic	Impaired thinking	Unknown irritability	Excessive Clinging	Increased question about beliefs/ God
Stomach aches	Nightmares/ Talking in sleep	Difficulty concentrating	Intensified startling response	May ask question of what a caregiver believes
Profuse sweating	Flashbacks can happen with sensory triggers	Rebellious / defiant	Demand of constant attention	Concerns that God has failed him.
Itchy / scratching	Impaired focus	Agitation	Return to old habits	Anger at God
vision changes / hearing complaints	Thinking thoughts or emotions are "crazy"	Severe panic		Moral compromise

AGES 11-14	AGES 11-14	AGES 11-14	AGES 11-14	AGES 11-14
PHYSICAL	**MENTAL**	**EMOTIONAL**	**BEHAVIOR**	**SPIRITUAL**
Fatigue /sleep changes	Blame someone	Insecure	Change activity	Inquires about spiritual things
Muscle tension	Poor Attention	Not wanting to go to school	Withdrawal	Question his basic beliefs
Skin changes / disorders	Poor Decisions	Aggression	Emotional outburst	Want to be around youth group
Bowel / digestive issues	Poor concentration	Withdrawn for friends	Suspicious / fearful /on alert	Uncharacteristic religious involvement
Change in eating habits. Over/ under eating	Alertness lower / raised	Fear	Change in communication/ confirms caregivers return	Sudden turn to or from God
Headaches	Memory problems	Uncertainty / Anxious	Restlessness	Inquires about Familial faith
Vomiting	Seeks confirming actions with expectations.	Emotional control challenges	May experiment with substance use as means of self medicating	Curious about God's power
Vision Problems	or awareness of surroundings	Depression	Self harm	Loss of meaning and purpose
Vague body aches	Poor problem solving ability	Disobedience / rebellious	Regressive behaviors	Feeling distant
Grinding Teeth	Nightmares	Apprehension	High demand of attention	Anger at clergy
Weakness	Impaired thinking	Overwhelmed	Won't do chores	Belief the God is not in control
Dizziness	Needs actions to align with communicated expectations.	Intense anger	Intensified startling response	God does not care
Profuse sweating	Increased worry	Irritability	Intensified startling response	Belief that failed God you
Chills	Impaired focus	Agitation	Random pacing	Anger at God
Shock Symptoms*	Concerned that his thoughts / emotions are "crazy"	Severe panic		Moral compromise

AGES 14 - 18	AGES 14 - 18	AGES 14 - 18	AGES 14 - 18	AGES 14 - 18
PHYSICAL	**MENTAL**	**EMOTIONAL**	**BEHAVIOR**	**SPIRITUAL**
Muscle tension	Blame someone	Anxiety	Change activity	Irritated by religions platitudes
Skin changes / disorders	Poor Attention	Guilt/ survivor guilt	Withdrawal	Question basic beliefs
Fatigue /sleep changes	Poor Decisions	Denial	Emotional outburst	Withdraw from place of worship
Painful menses	Poor concentration	May feel inadequate	Apprehensive	Uncharacteristic religious involvement
Startles easily	Skeptical	Increased / exaggerated Fear	Change in communication	Sudden turn from God
Bowel / digestive issues	Memory problems	Feelings of helpless	Restlessness	Familiar faith practice is empty
Change in eating habits. Over/ under eating	Self Esteem changes	Increased challenges concentrating	Substance use / abuse as means of self medicating	Belief that God is powerless
Headaches	or awareness of surroundings	Depression	Self harm at varied levels (get help)*	Loss of meaning and purpose
Vomiting	Poor problem solving ability	Powerful outbursts of emotions	Seek peer advice to cope.	Feeling distant
Vision Problems	Poor abstract thinking	Isolation / Withdrawn	Take increased risks	Anger at clergy
Vague body aches	Impaired thinking	Overwhelmed	Hyper alert to environment	Belief that God is not in control
Grinding Teeth	Nightmares	Intense anger	Intensified startling response	God does not care
Weakness	Flashbacks	May not care about outcomes	Intensified startling response	Belief that failed God you
Dizziness	Impaired focus	Agitation	Pacing	Anger at God / religion
Profuse sweating	Thinking thoughts or emotions are "crazy"	Panic attacks	increase /decreased sexual activity	Moral compromise from professed beliefs
Shock Symptoms*			May engage in sex to distract from unseen pain	

BIBLIOGRAPHY

BIBLES

International Bible Society. Holy Bible New International Version. Nashville TN. Zondervan Publishing. 1976.1978, 1984.

Green, Jay P. General Editor. The Interlinear Bible Hebrew-Greek-English. Hedrickson Publishers Edition. 1976, 1977, 1978, 1980, 1981, 1984.

Strong, James. *The Strongest Strong's Exhaustive Concordance Of The Bible.* Zondervan. Grand Rapids, MI. 2001.

Thompson, Frank Charles. *The Thompson Chain-Reference Bible New American Standard.* B.B.

Kirkbridge Bible Co. Indianapolis, IN. 1908, 1917, 1929, 1934, 1957, 1964, 1982, 1993.

SELECTED BIBLIOGRAPHY

Acosta, Judith, and Prager, Judith Simon. *The Worst Is Over: What To Say When Every Moment Counts — Verbal First Aid To Calm, Relieve Pain, Promote Healing, and Save Lives.* Jodre Group, Inc. San Diego, CA. 2002.

Andress, Vern R. "The Crisis of Suicide" in *Ministry; International Journal for Pastors*, vol. 69, no. 7. Hagerstown, MD. Seventh Day Adventist Ministerial Association, July 1996.

Ballard, Paul. *"Locating Chaplaincy: A Theological Note."* in Crucible July - September 2009.

Budson, Andrew E. *"Don't Listen To Your Lizard Brain"* in Psychology Today. December 3, 2017.

Bryan, C. J., Bryan, A. O., Roberge, E., Leifker, F. R., & Rozek, D. C., *"Moral injury, posttraumatic stress disorder, and suicidal behavior among National Guard personnel."* in Psychological Trauma: Theory, Research, Practice, and Policy, 10(1), 36-45. 2018. and https://doi.org/10.1037/tra0000290

Bryan, Craig J. AnnaBelle O. Bryan, Roberge Erika, Feea R. Leifker, and David C. Rozek. 2018. *"Moral Injury, Posttraumatic Stress Disorder, and Suicidal Behavior among National Guard Personnel."* in Psychological Trauma 10: 36–45.

Caperon, John. *"A Vital Ministry: Chaplaincy in Schools"* in The Post Christian Era. SCM Press, Golden Lane, London 2015.

Caperon, Caperon, John Todd, Andrew and Walters, James, editors. *A Christian Theology of Chaplaincy*. Jessica Kingsley Publisher, London, UK. 2018.

Carson, D. A. Carson. *The Gospel According to John* (Leicester: Apollos, 1991).

Cloud, Henry. *How To Have That Difficult Conversation: Gaining The Skills For Honest and Meaningful Communication*. Grand Rapids, MI. Zondervan. 2003.

———. *Changes That Heal: How To Understand Your Past To Ensure A Healthier Future*. Grand Rapids, MI. Zondervan. 2003.

———. *Necessary Endings: The Businesses and Relationship That All of Us Have To Give Up In Order To Move Forward*. New York, NY. Harper Business / Harper Collins. 2001.

Cloud, Henry and Townsend, John. *How People Grow: What The Bible Reveals About Personal Growth*. Grand Rapids, MI. 2001.

Currier, Joseph M., Kent D. Drescher, and Harris J. Irene. *"Spiritual Functioning among Veterans Seeking Residential Treatment for PTSD: A Matched Control Group Study."* in Spirituality in Clinical Practice 1: 3–15, 2014.

Currier, Joseph M., Jason M. Holland, and Kent D. Drescher. *"Spirituality Factors in the Prediction of Outcomes of PTSD Treatment for U.S. Military Veterans."* in Journal of Traumatic Stress 28: 57–64, 2015.

Cutcliffe, J., & Ball, P. B. (2009). *"Stakeholders Perspectives on Stigma of Suicide Attempt Survivors."* in Suicide Survivors and the Suicidology Academe: Reconciliation and reciprocity. Crisis. Sheehan, Lindsay L. Patrick Corrigan, Maya A. Al-Khouja, and the Stigma of Suicide Research Team. Hogrefe Publishing, Chicago, IL. 2016.

Duckman, Angela. Grit; The Power Of Passion And Perseverance. Scribner.An Imprint of Simon And Schuster of Ney York, NY. 2016.

Earp, Steven. *Storms of Life; Learning To Trust God Again.* Oklahoma City, OK. Elevate Faith. 2015.

Evans, Wyatt R., Melinda A. Stanley, Terri L. Barrera, Julie J. Exline, Kenneth I. Pargament, and Ellen J. Teng. *"Morally Injurious Events and Psychological Distress among Veterans: Examining the Mediating Role of Religious and Spiritual Struggles."* in Psychological Trauma 10: 360–67. 2018.

Exline, Julie J., Kenneth I. Pargament, Joshua B. Grubbs, and Ann Marie Yali. *"The Religious and Spiritual Struggles Scale: Development and Initial Validation."* in Psychology of Religion and Spirituality 6: 208–22. 2014.

Fanning, W. (1908). *"Chaplain."* in The Catholic Encyclopedia. New York: Robert Appleton Company. Retrieved February 10, 2018. from Advent: http://www.newadvent.org/cathen/03579b.htm

Farnsworth, J. K., Drescher, K. D., Nieuwsma, J. A., Walser, R. B., & Currier, J. M. (2014). *"The Role of Moral Emotions in Military Trauma: Implications for the Study and Treatment of*

Moral Injury." in Review of General Psychology, 18(4), 249-262, and https://doi.org/10.1037/gpr0000018

Figley, C. *"Compassion Fatigue: Coping with Secondary Traumatic Stress Disorder in Those Who Treat the Traumatized."* New York, NY: Brunner/Mazel. 1995.

FEMA, US Department of Homeland Security, *CERT Basic Training.* PerformTech, Inc. Alexandria, VA. 2001.

Frankfurt, Sheila, and Patricia Frazier. "A review of research on moral injury in combat veterans." in Military Psychology 28: 318–30. 2016.

Friedman, Matthew J., Patricia A. Resick, Richard A. Bryant, James Strain, Mardi Horowitz, and David Spiegel. *"Classification of Trauma and Stressor-related Disorders in DSM-5."* in Depression and Anxiety 28: 737–49. 2011.

Fuller, A. James. *Chaplain To The Confederacy.* Baton Rouge, Louisiana State University Press. 2000.

Galser, Barney, and Anselm L. Strauss. The Discovery of The Grounded Theory: Strategies for Qualitative Research. New York: Adeline de Gruyster. 1967.

Griffin, B. J., Purcell, N., Burkman, K., Litz, B. T., Bryan, C. J., Schmitz, M., Villierme, C., Walsh, J., & Maguen, S. (2019). *"Moral injury: An Integrative Review."* in Journal of Traumatic Stress, 32. (3), 350-362. 2019. and https://doi.org/10.1002/jts.22362

Grossman Lieutenant Colonel Dave. *On Killing: The Psychological Cost of Learning To Kill In War and Society.* New York, NY Bay Back Books / Little Brown and Company. 1995.

_____ and Christensen, Loren W. *On Combat: The Psychology and Physiology Of Deadly Conflict In War And Peace.* Mascoutah, IL. 2012.

Harris, J. Irene, Christopher R. Erbes, Brian E. Engdahl, Raymond H. A. Olson, Ann Marie

Winskowski, and Joelle McMahill. *"Christian Religious Functioning and Trauma Outcomes."* in Journal of Clinical Psychology 64: 17–29. 2008.

_____ Christopher R. Erbes, Engdahl,Brian E., Ogden, Henry, Raymond H. A. Olson, Ann Marie M. Winskowski, and Kelsey Campion SaariMataas. "Religious Distress and Coping With Stressful Life Events: A Longitudinal Study." in Journal of Clinical Psychology 68: 1276–86. 2012.

_____ Timothy, Usett, Voecks Cory, Thuras Paul, Currier Joseph, and Erbes Christopher. 2018. *"Spiritually Integrated Care for PTSD: A Randomized Controlled Trial of Building Spiritual Strength."* in Psychiatry Research 267: 420–28.

Hunt, June. *Seeing Yourself Through God's Eyes.* Eugene, OR. Harvest House Publishers. 2008.

———. *Biblical Counseling: Over 580 Real Life Topics More than 1,000 Relevant Verses.* Eugene, OR. Harvest House Publishers. 1973.

———. *Counseling Through Your The Bible Handbook: Providing Hope and Biblical Help For 50 Everyday Problems.* Harvest House Publishers. 2008.

_____. *Suicide Prevention; Hope When Life Seems Hopeless.* Dallas, TX. Hope International Publishing. 2017.

Initiative, Church. *Grief Share, Your Journey From Mourning to Joy.* Wake Forrest, NC. 1999.

Jeremiah, David. *Slaying The Giants In Your Life: You Can Win The Battle And Live Victoriously.* Thomas Nelson, Nashville, TN. 2001.

Lange D, Aart W, Neeleman J. *"The effect of the September 11 terrorist attacks on suicide and deliberate self-harm: a time trend study."* in Suicide Life Threat Behavior 34:439–447. 2004.

Leaf, Caroline. *Switch On Your Brain.* Baker Books. Grand Rapids, MI. 2013.

Leegood, Giles. *Chaplaincy: The Churches Sector Ministries*. London and New York: Cassell. 1999.

Litz, Brett T., Lebowitz Leslie, Matt J. Gray, and William P. Nash. 2015. *Adaptive Disclosure, A New Treatment for Military Trauma, Loss, and Moral Injury"*, 1st ed. New York: Guilford Publications M.U.A. 2017.

_____ Brett T., Stein Nathan, Delaney Eileen, Lebowitz Leslie, William P. Nash, Silva Caroline, and Maguen Shira. *"Moral Injury and Moral Repair in War Veterans: A Preliminary Model and Intervention Strategy."* in Clinical Psychology Review 29: 695–706. 2009.

Lusko, Levi. *I Declare War*. W. Publishing Group, Thomas Nelson. Nashville TN. 2018.

MacLean, Paul D. *"The Triune Brain in Evolution: Role"* in Paleoce-rebral Functions. New York, NY. Springer Publishing. 1990.

Maguen, Shira, and Matt A. Price. *"Moral Injury in the Wake of Coronavirus: Attending to the Psychological Impact of the Pandemic."* in Psychological Trauma 12: S131–S132. 2020.

Maxwell, John C. *Good Leaders Ask Great Questions: Your Foundation For Successful Leadership*. Hachette Book Group, New York, NY 2014.

Medenwald, Daniel. *"The Terror Attacks of 9/11 and Suicides in Germany: A Time Series Analysis."* in Medicine vol. 95,15. 2016.

Noel, Brook and Blair PhD., Pamela. *I Wasn't Ready To Say Goodbye: Surviving, Coping And Healing After Sudden Loss Of A Loved One*. Naperville, Illinois. Source book Inc. 2008.

Norman, S. B., Wilkins, K. C., Myers, U. S., & Allard, C. B. *"Trauma informed guilt reduction therapy with combat Veterans."* in Cognitive and Behavioral Practice, 21(1), 77-88. 2014. and https://doi.org/10.1016/j.cbpra.2013.08.001

Preus, Peter. *And She Was A Christian; Why Do Believers Commit Suicide?* Milwaukee, Wisconsin. Northwestern Publishing House. 2012.

Pulido, M.L. "*The Ripple Effect: Lessons Learned About Secondary Traumatic Stress Among Clinicians Responding to the September 11th Terrorist Attacks.*" in Clin Soc Work J 40, 307–315 (2012). https://doi.org/10.1007/s10615-012-0384-3

Purcell, N., Koenig, C. J., Bosch, J., & Maguen, S. "*Veterans' Perspectives on the Psychosocial Impact of Killing in War.*" in The Counseling Psychologist, 44(7), 1062-1099. 2016. and https://doi.org/10.1177/0011000016666156

Sanderberg, Sheryl and Grant, Adam. *Option B; Facing Adversity, Building Resilience, And Finding Joy.* Alfred A. Knopf A Division of Penguin Random House LLC., New York, NY. 2017.

Schuster MA, Stein BD, Jaycox L, et al. *A National Survey of Stress Reactions After the September 11, 2001, Terrorist Attacks.* in New England Journal of Medicine. 345:1507–1512. 2001.

Schwarz PhD., Arielle . *Complex PTSD Workbook: A Mind-Body Approach To Gaining Control & Becoming Whole.* Berkley. CA. Althea Press. 2016.

Sheehan, Lindsay L. Patrick Corrigan, Maya A. Al-Khouja, and the Stigma of Suicide Research Team. *Making Sense Of The Public Stigma Of Suicide: Factor Analyses Of Its Stereotypes, Prejudices, And Discriminations.* Hogrefe Publishing, Chicago, IL. 2016.

Sittser, Gerald L. *A Grace Disguised.* Grand Rapids, Michigan. Zondervan Publishing House. 1995.

Slater, Victoria. *Chaplaincy Ministry And The Mission Of The Church.* SCM Press, Golden Lane, London. 2015.

Steenkamp, Maria M., and Brett T. Litz."Psychotherapy for Military-related Posttraumatic Stress Disorder: Review of the Evidence." in Clinical Psychology Review 33: 45–53. 2013.

Swift, Christopher, Cobb, Mark and Todd, Andrew. Edited. *A Handbook of Chaplaincy Studies Understanding Spiritual Care In Public Places* Ashgate Contemporary Ecclesiology Series. Ashgate Publishing Company, Burlington, VT. 2015.

Tiede, Bob. *Great Leaders Ask Questions.* Leading With Questions, *leadingwithquestions.com/resources/.* May 2020.

_____ 339 Questions Jesus Asked. Leading With Questions, leadingwithquestions.com/resources/. May 2020.

Threllfall-Holmes, Miranda and Newitt, Mark. *Being A Chaplain.* SPCK Library of Ministry. 2011.

Vandecreek, Larry. Edited. *Professional Chaplaincy And Clinical Pastoral Education Should Become More Scientific: Yes and No.* The Haworth Pastoral Press, Binghamton, NY. 2002.

Van der Kolk, Cessen. *The Body Keeps The Score: Brain, Mind and Body In The Healing of Trauma.* New York, NY. Penguin Books. 2014.

Walton, Rus. Biblical Solutions For Contemporary Problems. Brentwood, TN Wolgemuth & Hyatt. 1988.

Westcott House *"Ministry Where People Are: A View Of Chaplaincy".* *Westcott House*; 2012 - 2013 in The Year In Review 2012 -2013.

Williams, Rowan. (2018). *"All Faiths and None?"* in A Christian Theology Of Chaplaincy. Edited by John Caperon, Andrew Todd, and James Walters. Jessica Kingsley Publisher, London, UK. (p.59 - p.78).

Wisco, Blair E., Brian P. Marx, Casey L. May, Brenda Martini, John H. Krystal, Steven M. Southwick, and Robert H. Pietrzak. *"Moral Injury in U.S. Combat Veterans: Results from the National Health and Resilience in Veterans Study."* in Depression and Anxiety 34: 340–47. 2017.

Wright, H. Norman. *Experience Grief.* Nashville, TN. B & H Publishing Group. 2004.

_____. *Helping Your Hurting Teens.* Torrence, CA. Aspire Press. 2014.

_____ *The Complete Book To Crisis and Trauma Counseling: What To Do And Say When It Matters Most.* Ventura, CA. Regal / From Gospel Light. 2011.

——-. *The New Guide To Crisis &Trauma Counseling: A Practical Guide for Ministers, Counselors and Lay Counselors.* Ventura, CA. Regal / From Gospel Light. 2003.

_____. *Quiet Times For Those Who Grieve.* Eugene, Oregon. Harvest House Publishing. 2005.

_____. *Recovering From Life's Losses.* Grand Rapids, MI. Fleming H. Revell. 1991.

_____. *Recovering For The Loss Of A Loved One.* Torrence, CA. Aspire Press. 2014.

_____. *Will I Ever Be The Same? Finding God's Strength To Hope Again.* Eugene Oregon. Harvest House Publishing. 2002.

Wright, H. Norman. Woodley, Matt and Julie. *Surviving The Storms Of Life; Finding Hope and Healing When Life Goes Wrong.* Grand Rapids Michigan, Revell a division of Baker Publishing Group. 2008.

Zeiglar PhD, Dave. *Traumatic Experience And The Brain: A Handbook For Understanding and Treating Those Traumatized As Children.* Jasper, OR. SCAR / Jasper Mountain. 2002.

Ziglar, Zig. *Confessions Of A Grieving Christian.* Nashville, TN. Broadman & Holman Publishers. 2004.

Ziglar, Zig and Ziglar, Tom. *Born To Win: Finding Your Success Code.* Dallas, TX. Success Books. 2012.

Zimmermann, Peter, Christian Fischer, Sebastian Lorenz, and Alliger-Horn Christina. *"Changes of personal values in deployed German Armed Forces Soldiers with psychiatric disorders."* in Wehrmedizinische Monatsschrift 60: 7–14. 2016.

ONLINE PUBLICATIONS

Allen, Bob, *"Family Says Seminary Professor's Death a Suicide"* Baptist New Global SEPTEMBER 9, 2015. https://baptistnews.com/article/family-says-professor-s-death-a-suicide/#.X4sO-Jy9h2uU

American Addiction Centers. "Anniversary Reactions to a Traumatic Event: The Recovery Continues" in An American Addiction Resource. SAMHSA. 2002. https://www.mentalhelp.net/ptsd/anniversary-reactions-to-a-traumatic-event/

Cafasso, Jacquelyn, "Traumatic Events," July 8, 2017, in Healthline Media 2020. https://www.healthline.com/health/traumatic-events#seeking-help

Catechism Of The Catholic Church http://www.vatican.va/archive/ccc_css/archive/catechism/p3s2c2a5.htm

Center For Disease Control "*Suicide Statistics at a Glance Fact Shee*t." 2015. on https://www.cdc.gov/violenceprevention/pdf/suicide-datasheet-a.pdf

Norman, Sonya B. PhD and Maguen, Shira PhD *"What Is Moral Injury?"* inPTSD: National Center For PTSD, U.S. Department of Veterans Affairs, NW Washington DC, May 19, 2020. https://www.ptsd.va.gov/professional/treat/cooccurring/moral_injury.asp

Office of Mental Health. *"Anniversary Reactions to a Traumatic Event: The Recovery Process Continues."* in Office of Mental Health, NY. 2020. http://omh.ny.gov/omhweb/disaster_resources/pandemic_influenza/anniversary_reactions_to_traumatic_event.html

ScienceNetLinks, *"Organ Systems, Nervous System."* Advanced Science Assisting Society, AAAS 2020. http://sciencenetlinks.com/student-teacher-sheets/organ-systems/

Segall, Laurie *"Suicides May Be Linked To Ashley Madison Hack"* in CNN Business, August 25, 2015. https://money.cnn.com/2015/08/24/technology/suicides-ashley-madison/index.html?iid=EL

Segall, Laurie, *"Pastor Outed On Ashley Madison Commits Suicide"* in CNN Business, September 8, 2015. https://money.cnn.

com/2015/09/08/technology/ashley-madison-suicide/index. html

Smith III , Julius , W3K Publishing , 2010 https://ccrma.stanford. edu/~jos/pasp/Newton_s_Three_Laws_Motion.html

Stone, Deb ScD, MSW, MPH, *"Violence Prevention: Suicide,"* Center for Disease Control and Prevention, September 8, 2020. https://www.cdc.gov/violenceprevention/suicide/index.html

The University of North Carolina at Charlotte ,*"What is Post Trauma Growth?"* Department of Psychology University North Carolina. 2014. https://ptgi.uncc.edu/what-is-ptg/

Vitelli, Romeo PhD *"PTSD in Survivors of 9/11 New research explores PTSD and depression in 9/11 survivors"* in Psychology Today, Oct 15, 2018. https://www.psychologytoday.com/us/ blog/media-spotlight/201810/ptsd-in-survivors-911

Scripture Index

Old Testament

Genesis 3:1 53
Genesis 3:15 175

Exodus 17:10-12 161
Exodus 20:5-6 154
Exodus 22:3 126

Deuteronomy 5:17 133
Deuteronomy 6:5 52
Deuteronomy 26:17-19 46

Joshua 5:13-15 194
Joshua 6:27 196
Joshua 24:15 155

Judges 9:54 136, 185
Judges 16:28 181
Judges 16:30 136

1 Samuel 31:4 136
1Samuel 31:5 136

2 Samuel 17:23 185
2 Samuel 17:33 136
2 Samuel 22:6 183
2 Samuel 23:13 181

1 Kings 16:18 136
1 Kings 19:4 161

1 Kings 19:9 181

2 Kings 17:32 175

1 Chronicles 10:4 185
1 Chronicles 10:5 185

2 Chronicles 7:14 39
2 Chronicles 20:33 34

Nehemiah 4:16-18 49

Psalm 10:4 35
Psalm 27:1 175
Psalm 31:9 181
Psalm 41:1 139
Psalm 42:11 169
Psalm 50:12 195
Psalm 55:5 184
Psalm 62:5 133
Psalm 127:1 155
Psalm 139:13, 16 133
Psalm 139:143 181

Proverbs 1:5 139, 155
Proverbs 3:5-6 139, 194
Proverbs 4:10 179
Proverbs 4:20 139
Proverbs 4:25 155
Proverbs 6:25 54

Proverbs 11:13 139
Proverbs 11:14 154
Proverbs 13:12 169
Proverbs 14:12 54
Proverbs 14:15 155
Proverbs 15:4 139
Proverbs 15:22 153
Proverbs 15:28 139
Proverbs 16:1-3 139
Proverbs 16:3 155
Proverbs 16:21 172
Proverbs 16:24 139
Proverbs 17:17 139
Proverbs 18:24 74
Proverbs 20:19 139
Proverbs 21:10-12 172
Proverbs 23:7 158
Proverbs 25:11 139
Proverbs 27:3 124
Proverbs 27:5 125
Proverbs 27:6 125
Proverbs 27:17 138
Proverbs 29:25 185
Proverbs 30:20 36

Ecclesiastes 4:11 139
Ecclesiastes 4:12 139
Ecclesiastes 8:5-7 155
Ecclesiastes 9:16-18 147

Isaiah 14:11-13 52
Isaiah 42:3 68
Isaiah 50:2 59
Isaiah 55:8 194
Isaiah 58:6-7 39
Isaiah 58:9-14 39
Isaiah 58:14 40
Isaiah 59: 1-2 59
Isaiah 59:4 59

Jeremiah 7:9 129
Jeremiah 17:9-10 158

Jeremiah 17:10 159
Jeremiah 17:14 133
Jeremiah 29:11 133
Jeremiah 29:13 154
Jeremiah 33:3 8

Lamentations 3:19-20 180

Ezekiel 28:2 36
Ezekiel 33:1-6 63
Ezekiel 33:31 35

Haggai 1:2 36

Zechariah 11:12-13 122, 125

NEW TESTAMENT

Matthew 4:1 54
Matthew 7:26 36
Matthew 12:30-32 127
Matthew 16:33 178
Matthew 22:37-39 37
Matthew 24:14 57
Matthew 26:14-15 123
Matthew 26:21 124
Matthew 26:24-25 122
Matthew 26:50 74
Matthew 27:5 125, 136
Matthew 27:5-10 126

Mark 3:28 127
Mark 4:23 154

Luke 4:1 54
Luke 9:62 155
Luke 14:18 37

John 8:32 154
John 8:44 53
John 10:27-30 59

John 15:13 68
John 17 71
John 17:9-12. 56
John 17:12 62
John 17:13-21 72
John 19:30 53

Acts 1:18 125, 126
Acts 3:17 174
Acts 5 147
Acts 9:4 8
Acts 10:34-36 27
Acts 17:29-31 162
Acts 17:30 126, 150, 174

Romans 3:23 52, 176
Romans 8:1-8 157
Romans 8:28 133, 173
Romans 8:29 134
Romans 11:29 173
Romans 12:1 134
Romans 12:2 34, 191
Romans 12:4-5 134

1 Corinthians 6:19 133
1 Corinthians 6:20 56, 68
1 Corinthians 10:13 54, 60, 154
1 Corinthians 15:54-56 52

2 Corinthians 2:10-11 54
2 Corinthians 5:21 56
2 Corinthians 6:16 36
2 Corinthians 7:9-12 167
2 Corinthians 10:3-5 50, 193
2 Corinthians 11:13-15 52
2 Corinthians 13:5 34

Ephesians 6:11-17 50

Philippians 4:6-7 133
Philippians 4:8 168

Colossians 3: 9-14 31
Colossians 3:11 33

1 Timothy 2:6 68
1 Timothy 5:8 64

2 Timothy 1:6 177
2 Timothy 1:7 168, 175
2 Timothy 2:15-17a 68
2 Timothy 4:3-4 176

Hebrew 5:12-14 51
Hebrews 1:8-14 17
Hebrews 3:15 36
Hebrews 6:12 35
Hebrews 7:21-22 168
Hebrews 12:1 51
Hebrews 12:1-3 55
Hebrews 12:9-11 38
Hebrews 12:11 34
Hebrews 12:25 35

James 2:18-20 55
James 4:14 36

1 Peter 1:13 171
1 Peter 2:2-3 51
1 Peter 3:15 103
1 Peter 5:8 53

2 Peter 1:2-8 45
2 Peter 1:3-4 133
2 Peter 1:5-8 150
2 Peter 1:5-9 7
2 Peter 1:8-9 151
2 Peter 3:9 59

1 John 4:18 168

Jude 9 58

Revelation 2:23 159

Revelation 3:12 57
Revelation 3:15-16 32
Revelation 5:59 33
Revelation 7:9 33
Revelation 12:8-10 56
Revelation 12:10 23, 53
Revelation 12:10-12 169
Revelation 12:11 57

www.ingramcontent.com/pod-product-compliance
Lightning Source LLC
Chambersburg PA
CBHW031505270326
41930CB00006B/261